Building

DOORS & DRAWERS

A Complete Guide to Design and Construction

Building
DOORS & DRAWERS
A Complete Guide to Design and Construction

Dovetailed Drawers • Utility Drawers • Cabinet Doors • Special Doors • Hardware

The Taunton Press

The Taunton Press
Inspiration for hands-on living®

The Taunton Press, Inc., 63 South Main Street, PO Box 5506, Newtown, CT 06470-5506
e-mail: tp@taunton.com

Editor: Paul Anthony
Jacket/Cover design: Guilio Turturro
Interior design: Susan Fazekas
Layout: Susan Fazekas
Illustrator: Christopher Mills
Photographer: Andy Rae (except where noted)

Library of Congress Cataloging-in-Publication Data
Rae, Andy.
  Building doors & drawers : a complete guide to design and construction / Andy Rae.
    p. cm.
  ISBN 978-1-56158-868-8
  1. Cabinetwork. 2. Built-in furniture. 3. Wooden doors. I. Title. II. Title: Building doors and drawers.

TT197.R285 2007
684.1'6--dc22

2007009001

Printed in the United States of America
10 9 8 7 6 5 4 3 2 1

The following manufacturers/names appearing in *Building Doors & Drawers* are trademarks:
Panalign Strips®, Spaceballs®

Working wood is inherently dangerous. Using hand or power tools improperly or ignoring safety practices can lead to permanent injury or even death. Don't try to perform operations you learn about here (or elsewhere) unless you're certain they are safe for you. If something about an operation doesn't feel right, don't do it. Look for another way. We want you to enjoy the craft, so please keep safety foremost in your mind whenever you're in the shop.

Thanks

Like any text on woodworking, this book exists thanks to the community of woodworkers in my life. Some are long gone; some are very much present. They include my personal woodworking pals, woodworkers I admire from afar, the many woodworking tool manufacturers that supply us with the means to work the material, my fellow woodworking journalists, and a select editorial crew at Taunton. It is the sum total of all these people that ultimately provides the information that becomes a book about making something, in this case doors and drawers. I am simply a filter through which this information passes, coloring the story with my own personal woodworking experience. The truth is, without the support and wisdom of countless woodworkers and wood aficionados, as well as the daily connection to my family, I would be less of a woodworker and couldn't possibly dream of being an author. So thanks—to everyone. You are all needed and admired more than you know.

—Andy Rae, 2007

Part One

DRAWERS

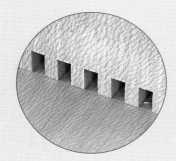

Part Two

DOORS

Introduction

Drawers hold secrets, and doors open to reveal wonders worth seeking. These are some of the attributes that make doors and drawers worth building. Perhaps more compelling is the fact that, without doors and drawers, a cabinet is simply an open reservoir subject to dust and dirt, accumulated piles of inaccessible junk, and to prying eyes. Doors and drawers help keep our treasures clean, concealed, and organized, preserving the mystery of our lives while making them more practical.

On a functional level, a door or drawer must operate smoothly to provide easy access into a cabinet. Solid construction, a good fit, and the proper hinge or opening system are all parts of the puzzle that must come together for your project's success. Put these things together and your drawers and doors will never droop, stick, or squeak.

There's an aesthetic value to reap as well because a cabinet's doors and drawers are its most visible parts. Walk into any room and you'll immediately detect the flavor of the cabinet that lives there by the style of its doors and drawers. Nowhere else on a case does an element take up as much space or offer as important a look. This makes the design of your doors and drawers a vital element to the success of your furniture. Luckily, there's an endless variety of shapes and styles to choose from, and much to consider if you want to make good-looking doors and drawers.

All this information and more can be found inside this book. To make it as accessible as possible, I've divided the book into two sections. Part One is all about drawer making. It includes the various styles of drawers, the types of cabinets they'll fit, the types of joints used to construct them, and how to assemble, fit, and finish them so they slide like a whisper in and out of your case. There's also plenty of information about choosing and using handles and pulls, as well as installing locks and drawer stops. There's even a chapter on special drawers, the kind that add value or utility and elevate your work from the ordinary to the extraordinary.

Part Two dives into the world of making doors. It's organized in a fashion similar to Part One,

presenting styles and types of doors, and methods for fitting them to their cabinets. I'll discuss the types of joints used to build doors and how to fit and hang them, including what hardware to use and what type of latch or knob is most appropriate. There's also a chapter devoted to special doors—ones that depart from the norm. Making these doors will challenge your skills, expand your woodworking horizons, and make your cabinets shine brighter.

So dig in. There's plenty to learn. Look at the pictures, read the text, practice the techniques, and try a few designs. Soon you'll be making quality doors and heirloom drawers. And don't worry—you won't need an exotic collection of tools or a master's hand to get good results. The craft of door and drawer making is well within your grasp if you take it step by step. My hope is that, with a little patience and a lot of practice, you'll learn how to build beautiful, functional doors and drawers that will live comfortably in their cases while serving you for many years to come.

1 DESIGNING DRAWERS

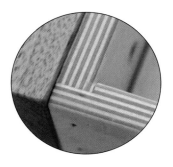

You may have a favorite drawer. You know, the one that feels good in the hand when you grasp its handle and begin to pull. Even when filled with prized goods, it slides out easily and with authority, running smoothly and never snagging or tipping down more than a smidgeon. You may even find the sound of its movement appealing, whether it's the *whizzz* of a pair of engineered metal channels rolling along dozens of tiny steel balls, or the more subtle *snick* of wood gliding on wood. And it closes softly, without complaint.

This part of the book is designed to help you make drawers that you'll love. To get started, you'll first want to choose the style of drawer you want to use, whether overlay, half-overlay, or flush. You'll need to decide whether to use a wood-to-wood mounting system (where the drawer is guided by wooden parts of the case), or whether to mount them using commercial metal slides. You'll also want to proportion the parts properly so they work well and look great, and you'll need to choose the appropriate materials, joinery, and finish. All these design choices will impact how your drawers will look and, more important, they'll help you make a drawer that operates flawlessly for years to come.

Drawer Styles

Take your pick. There are three main styles of drawers: overlay, half-overlay, and flush. The style you select greatly impacts the look of your cabinet front, so that's where you should first focus your energy (see the drawing on p. 6).

Overlay drawers have become associated with the 32mm cabinet industry. What was once an exclusively European style has migrated stateside to become a standard modern design for kitchen and bath cabinetry. With this style, drawers and doors are placed close together with only small gaps, or reveals, between them. This creates the uncluttered appearance of a single face across the entire front of the cabinets.

HANGING OUT. An overlay drawer sports a face that lays over the front of the case and meets neighboring components within about ⅛ in., creating consistent small gaps, or reveals, all around the perimeter.

TYPES OF DRAWERS

Overlay

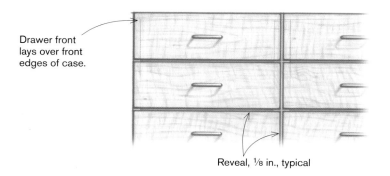

Drawer front lays over front edges of case.

Reveal, 1/8 in., typical

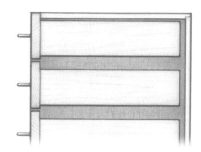

Lipped

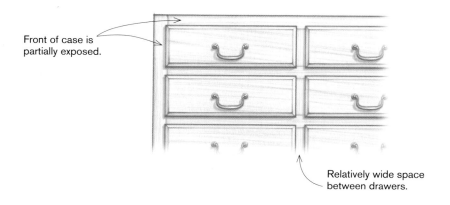

Front of case is partially exposed.

Relatively wide space between drawers.

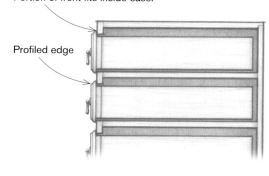

Portion of front fits inside case.

Profiled edge

Flush or Inset

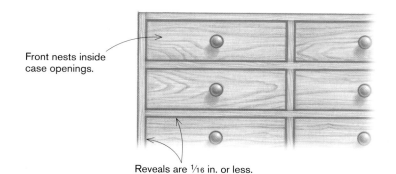

Front nests inside case openings.

Reveals are 1/16 in. or less.

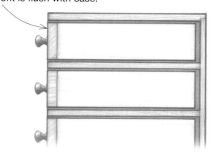

Front is flush with case.

Half Inset

Front is set back slightly into case.

Half-overlay drawers, also called *lipped* drawers, add more detail to the front of a cabinet, especially when the lipping itself is profiled. The design works well with both modern and traditional cabinetry. This type of drawer can be one of the easiest to fit, since the lipped front hides the gap between the drawer box and case, and the spaces between neighboring drawers and doors are relatively wide. Keep in mind that the front of the cabinet—with or without a face frame—becomes a more visible component when using this style, so select your frame or case stock carefully so it looks good behind your drawers.

Flush drawers, also called *inset* drawers, are fussier to fit and often more challenging to build. However, the payoff is a clean, fitted look like no other. With the face of the drawer and the face of the case in the same plane, and with the tight, consistent reveals around its edges, a flush drawer emanates the feel of fine craftsmanship. The Shakers used this type of drawer to great advantage, outfitting entire walls in a room with rows upon rows of drawers all painstakingly nested into their respective openings. Somewhat less demanding to build is a half-inset drawer, which either protrudes or sets back slightly from the case. This adds shadow-line detail while minimizing the need to create perfectly consistent reveals.

Drawer Anatomy

A drawer is basically a box without a lid. It consists of a front, a back, two sides, and a bottom (see the drawing on p. 8). For purposes of our discussion here, let's refer to the front, back, and sides as the "walls" of the box.

When making drawers from solid wood (I'll discuss plywood in a bit), it's important to orient the grain of the walls so it runs around the drawer, parallel to its top and bottom edges. That way, the parts expand and contract uniformly, maintaining joint integrity. The walls can be joined at the

LIP HIDES THE GAP. Half-overlay drawers work well on traditional case pieces, adding visual detail while concealing any gaps between the drawer box and the case.

CLOSE TOLERANCES. Inset drawers demand careful fitting to create consistent reveals, but the result is a clean look that reflects fine craftsmanship.

corners in a variety of ways, which I'll delve into in Chapter 2. The "show" drawer front, made of your featured wood, can be joined directly to the drawer sides, or you can make a separate "applied" front, and simply screw it to an independently made drawer box during installation. (See Chapter 3.)

It's important to consider the patterning and coloring of the stock you use for your "show" drawer

DRAWER ANATOMY

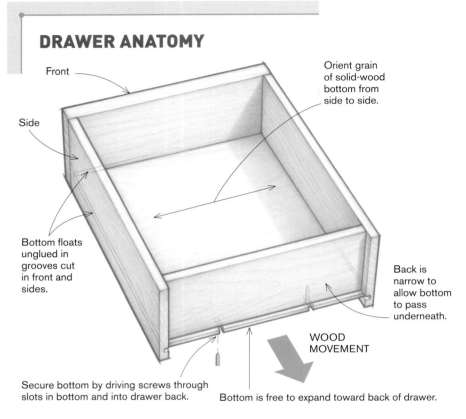

Front

Side

Orient grain of solid-wood bottom from side to side.

Bottom floats unglued in grooves cut in front and sides.

Back is narrow to allow bottom to pass underneath.

WOOD MOVEMENT

Secure bottom by driving screws through slots in bottom and into drawer back.

Bottom is free to expand toward back of drawer.

fronts. Whenever possible, take the time to lay out your stock so adjacent drawer fronts will be cut in sequence from the same board. The visual effect is much more harmonious than using randomly placed boards for drawer fronts.

In traditional drawer construction, the drawer back is made narrower and sits above the drawer bottom. This is necessary to allow for wood movement when using solid wood drawer bottoms, which were prevalent before the advent of commonly available plywood. Although using plywood avoids problems with wood movement, solid wood drawer bottoms add a touch of class, and are often a good choice for high-end work.

When fitting a solid wood bottom panel, make sure to orient it so the grain runs parallel to the drawer front. That way, the unglued panel can expand toward the back of the drawer without ill effect. Otherwise, a panel that swells side to side can bind a drawer in its opening or even break its

FOLLOW THE GRAIN. For a harmonious look, these drawer fronts were milled from the same tree. Just as important, adjacent drawer fronts were sequentially cut from the same board, creating continuously flowing grain across the entire cabinet face.

ONE-WAY GRAIN. Always orient a solid-wood bottom so its grain runs from side to side. Screws installed through slots sawn on the tablesaw and into the drawer back allow the panel to move toward the back of the drawer as it expands.

corner joints. Solid wood drawer bottoms can be milled to any thickness, coving or rabbeting them at the edges to fit into their grooves if necessary.

With plywood drawer bottoms, wood movement isn't an issue because the material is stable. In fact, one of the best-kept "secrets" to using plywood for drawer bottoms is that you can glue the bottom into its drawer box grooves, thereby greatly improving the overall strength of the drawer itself, as I'll discuss in Chapter 2.

Proportioning a Drawer

Dimensioning drawers properly includes more than simply building to fit an opening. For a drawer to operate well, consider the ratio of its width to length. In general, the longer the drawer, the better it will track. If it's too wide, it will tend to rack in its opening. You'll also want to avoid overly tall drawers. Wide, solid-wood fronts and sides can expand enough to jam in their openings, and deep drawers typically waste space. There are no hard rules here, but when you get the chance, it's usually better to divide a cabinet into multiple drawer openings to reduce each individual drawer's width or height.

Another rule of proportioning is to keep the sides and backs of your drawers thin. This is mostly an aesthetic decision. Thick-sided drawers look and feel clunky when you open them, especially when the sides are the same thickness as the front. In general, you shouldn't need more than about ½ in. of thickness in a drawer side for it to run smoothly and track well, even if the drawer is only supported by its two sides, as is the case with wood-to-wood drawers. Adding a thicker front (typically ¾ in. to 1 in.) results in a pleasing proportion and provides enough thickness for sound corner joints.

THIN IS IN. Drawers with sides thinner than their fronts will track just fine in their openings while offering a pleasing proportion to the eye.

GOOD PROPORTIONS

For a drawer to track well and look good, pay attention to its overall size and the proportioning of its parts.

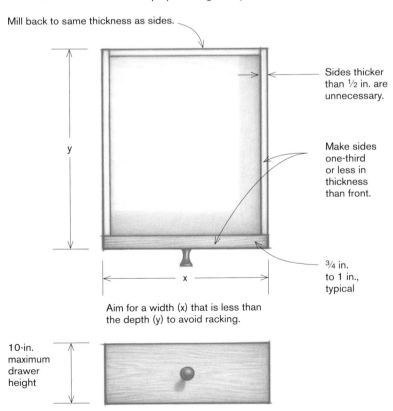

Mill back to same thickness as sides.

Sides thicker than ½ in. are unnecessary.

Make sides one-third or less in thickness than front.

¾ in. to 1 in., typical

y

x

Aim for a width (x) that is less than the depth (y) to avoid racking.

10-in. maximum drawer height

Selecting Drawer Stock

Not all wood is suitable for drawers, so it pays to select your stock carefully. In general, hardwoods are the best choice for drawer sides because they wear better than softwoods. Of course, if you're making small drawers that won't be holding much weight, such as those found in a keepsake box, then softer woods might work well enough. But for most drawer applications, a hard, strong, and stable wood is your best choice.

An alternative is to use plywood for drawer sides. Because of its stability and availability in wide form, it's a particularly good choice for tall drawers. However, please refrain from using particleboard or MDF (medium-density fiberboard) for drawer stock. While these sheet goods are widely used by the commercial cabinetmaking industry, the fact is they're a poor choice for drawers, as they don't have the necessary grain structure for sound corner joints, nor do they hold up well when exposed to moisture.

As discussed previously, drawer bottoms can be made of solid wood or plywood. If wide solid stock isn't available, you can glue-up narrow boards to make the necessary width for drawer bottoms. Because of its ready availability in wide panel form, plywood is a great choice for drawer bottoms, especially for utilitarian cabinetry.

Solid wood

Although you might choose a highly figured wood for a drawer front to dress up the face of a cabinet, it's best to use mild-grained stock for the sides and back. Use stable wood to prevent warping, which can cause a box to bind in its opening. It's also best to use clear stock with no knots, cracks, or blemishes.

To ensure that drawer sides stay straight and flat over time, it's common practice to use quartersawn stock. This is simply wood that has been cut from the log so that the annular rings are oriented at about 90 degrees to the face of the board. A long-standing favorite among woodworkers is quartersawn white oak, which has the benefits of both stability and good wear resistance.

Be careful when selecting quartersawn stock, though. Many "quartered" woods—especially the oaks—display large patches of medullary rays, which are thin and brittle, and can flake or chip during drawer operation, leaving rough spots on a drawer. To avoid this problem, you can choose riftsawn wood, where the annular rings are oriented roughly 45 degrees to the face. Like quartered wood, riftsawn stock is straight-grained on its face and more stable than plainsawn. However, the rays take the form of compact lines instead of patches, and won't chip away from the surface.

Don't overlook the fact that certain woods can impart pleasant aromas to your work and deter unwanted guests in the bargain. For example, making drawer bottoms from cedar of Lebanon or Spanish cedar will impart a delicious scent while repelling moths and other insects.

INSPECT THE ENDS. The annular growth rings on the quarter-sawn white oak board at left run perpendicular to its broad face, while the rings on a plainsawn board at right form a series of arcs running nearly parallel to the face.

Plywood

Hardwood plywood is an excellent material for many types of drawers. (Softwood plywood, used in building construction, is too ratty for the purpose and should be avoided.) In addition to drawer bottoms, plywood can be used for drawer walls and fronts. Available in large panels, it offers an efficient way to make big, stable drawer parts. Plywood drawers won't suffer from seasonal wood movement, jamming in their openings or creating large, unsightly gaps. That said, plywood is not a good choice for drawer sides that will need trimming for final fitting, as with a wood-to-wood-mounted drawer. But it can be a very economical material to use for drawers hung with commercial drawer slides.

Be aware that not all plywood is created equal. Standard hardwood plywood, conveniently available at many home supply stores, will work for drawers, but it's not very consistent in its quality. The ½-in.-thick panels usually consist of only five or seven plies, with the face veneers being very thin. The interior plies may include voids, which can show up at the edges of cut pieces.

There are better grades of plywood, though you may need to purchase them through specialty lumber dealers. For lack of an actual industry term, I call these "premium" or "multi-ply" plywoods. Some are sold under the names *Baltic birch* or *Apple ply*, but there are others as well. The primary distinguishing characteristics of these premium plywoods are that they have more plies than standard plywood and are free of internal voids. Overall, they are stiffer and denser than standard plywood. They hold fasteners better and make for stronger joints. And, being void-free, you can smooth their raw edges for a finished look.

Another advantage is that these premium plywoods are available in prefinished sheets, with a tough, catalyzed coating on one or both faces. This can save you a lot of time, since your drawer box won't need finishing after assembly.

However, avoid using prefinished plywood for drawer sides that will rub against wood, such as a wood-to-wood drawer, or choose a panel that's been finished on one side only and orient that side inside the drawer box. The commercial finish used on these sheets is too heavy, and you'll risk the drawer sticking in its opening if a finished side rubs against the cabinet.

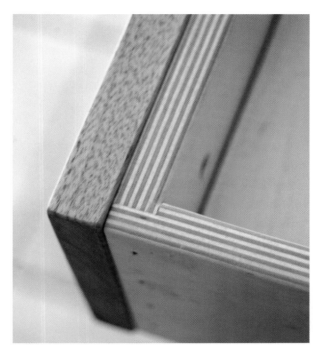

MULTIPLE PLIES LOOK GOOD. Multiply plywood, such as Baltic birch, is stiff and strong and without internal voids, making it a good choice for drawer parts with visible edges.

FINISHED BEFORE YOU BUILD IT. Using prefinished sheets of multi-ply plywood lets you dimension drawer parts, cut the joints, and assemble the drawer without having to apply a finish later.

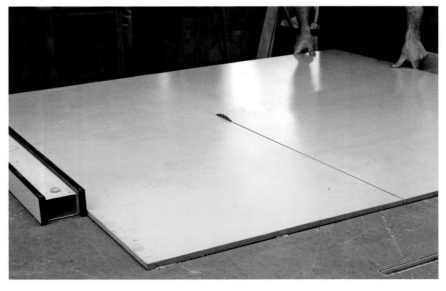

Choosing Commercial Slides

Commercial metal slides are generally used for utilitarian cabinetry, and you may think they don't belong in fine furniture. However, modern slides have come a long way in the past decade or so. Some of today's choices offer silky, whisper-quiet action, virtual invisibility, and minute-quick installation.

There are two primary styles of metal slides: side mount and undermount. Side-mount slides are the least expensive and the easiest to install. They come in left and right pairs for each drawer, and each slide consists of two parts: a runner, which is screwed to the drawer side, and a housing for the runner that you screw inside the case. A close cousin, the corner-mount slide, works along the same principle, with a runner that screws to the sides as well as wrapping under its bottom edge for increased load-bearing capacity.

Side-mount slides are available in bare metal versions that run in ball-bearing housings, or in colored, epoxy-coated varieties that incorporate nylon wheels. The nylon-wheel slides are generally quieter, but only the ball-bearing types are available as full-extension slides, permitting easy access to the contents at the back of a drawer. For even greater access, you can use "over-travel" slides, which allow even greater extension, making them a good choice for drawers directly beneath an overhang such as a kitchen countertop. Keep in mind that these specialty slides cost more.

The biggest recent innovation in the drawer slide industry is the refinement of "undermount" slides. Formerly clunky, tricky-to-install, two-part hardware, these used to require interior bracing at the back of the cabinet and provided a tenuous connection at best. Now, however, undermount slides are available as no-fuss, single-part slides that mount easily into the case, engage the drawer via a clip or a small hole drilled in the drawer, and run easily and dependably like a German motorcycle. The more expensive models even have a spring-actuated mechanism that pulls the drawer in quietly and securely once you've given it a gentle push.

AFFORDABLE AND EASY TO USE. Standard metal slides, such as these corner-mount versions, are quick to install and won't break the bank when you have a lot of drawers to hang.

NOW YOU SEE IT . . . These undermount slides are screwed to the case and engage the drawer via a clip mounted under the drawer bottom. Once installed, you don't see any hardware, and a cleverly designed spring mechanism closes the drawer for you.

Planning for the Finish

Smoothing and applying a finish to your drawers can be a chore if you don't plan for it. Using pre-finished parts can reduce the tedium, but that's not always an option depending upon the design of the drawer. However, you always have the choice of adding the drawer bottom at a later stage of construction. (See Chapter 2: Building Drawers.) This can help in several ways.

First, with the bottom removed, you have better access for gripping the drawer as you smooth and refine its surfaces. For example, you can clamp a solid-wood drawer box in a vise or hang it on a board that's cantilevered off the bench top to trim and smooth exterior surfaces readily.

It's also easier to apply a hand-rubbed finish to the walls of a drawer box without the bottom installed. Inside corners are more accessible, and the bottom itself can be finished as a separate panel without fear of drips or excess build-up in corners. One word of caution: Don't use oils or varnishes inside your drawers, or inside any casework, for that matter. Fumes from these finishes will give off an unpleasant odor for years to come, and can contaminate contents, especially cloth goods.

Lacquer works well enough, and it is often used by commercial shops to finish drawers. However, in an enclosed area like this, it can emit an odor for some weeks, so you might want to wait until it cures totally before putting the drawer into service. My favorite interior finish is dewaxed shellac, which can be wiped, brushed, or sprayed on. It's easy to apply, odorless once it dries (which takes only minutes), and imparts a warm glow to any wood.

NO BOTTOM IN THE WAY. With the bottom removed, you can easily clamp a drawer box to the bench for smoothing and fitting tasks.

WIPE ON WITH EASE. Applying a hand-rubbed finish is much easier without the bottom in place, letting you get into corners without fretting. And the bottom itself can be finished as a separate piece for a smoother finish.

2 BUILDING DRAWERS

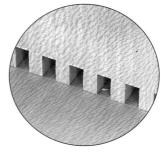

- *Building a Case for Drawers*
- *Drawer Construction*
- *Rabbet, Dado, and Box Joints*
- *Dovetails*
- *Drawer Assembly*

Once you've settled on a particular drawer design, consider how it will move in and out of the cabinet, which tells you the type of case or furniture frame to build. The easiest tracking method is to use metal slide hardware, but many woodworkers like to make their own drawer guide systems. The traditional approach is to make a case that accommodates a "wood-on-wood" drawer, whereby the drawer itself rides on wooden bearing surfaces in the case. This is a demanding type of drawer and cabinet to build, but the result is elegant and speaks of fine woodworking.

Choose your joinery carefully when making a drawer. Drawers are subject to stress as they're pulled in and out of a case, so the drawer box itself, especially the corner joints, must be sound and well made. And parts must come together flat and square to ease the job of fitting the drawer and to ensure that it tracks well in its drawer opening.

Building a Case for Drawers

Before cutting any drawer parts, first decide how you're going to guide the drawer in and out of the case or furniture frame so you can build the case accordingly. There are essentially two choices: using metal slides, or building a drawer that rides on wooden parts in the case, which I call a "wood-to-wood" drawer. Regardless of the type of tracking system you use, it's important to build the case or frame first, so you can build your drawers to exacting dimensions that will fit the openings.

Using commercial metal slides makes the job of building the cabinet and installing drawers a snap. Your cabinet doesn't need any special fitments, other than perhaps a shim or two to align the slides and drawers with the case opening. And you won't have the chore of fitting the drawer once it's constructed. Simply screw the slides to the drawer and case, pop the drawer in the case, and you're good to go. Slides can be used with either plywood or solid-wood cases, though they're typically found in plywood kitchen-cabinet construction.

QUICK INSTALLATION. Simply align metal slides with the edges of the drawer opening, shimming them out where necessary, as when accommodating an overhanging face frame. Screw them in place, and you're done.

A wood-to-wood drawer and the case that houses it can be more intricate to engineer. The drawer itself must be made to close tolerances, and outfitting the case with guides requires either

GROOVED TO GO. Rout a stopped groove in the sides of the drawer, mount a wooden runner in the case and you have a smooth method of travel—and a built-in drawer stop to boot.

RIDING ON BLOCKS. On frame pieces such as tables, L-shaped blocks support the drawer, guiding the bottom and sides. Glue and screw a block to each opposing apron, notching its ends if necessary to fit around the legs.

DRAWERS SLIDE WHILE CASE MOVES. Web frames built into the case support the drawers on wooden runners while allowing solid-wood case sides to swell and shrink with the seasons.

BUILDING A WEB FRAME

Elongated screw holes and floating tenons at the rear of the frame allow solid-wood sides to expand and contract freely.

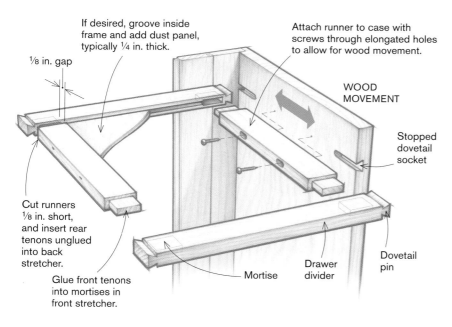

If desired, groove inside frame and add dust panel, typically ¼ in. thick.

⅛ in. gap

Attach runner to case with screws through elongated holes to allow for wood movement.

WOOD MOVEMENT

Stopped dovetail socket

Cut runners ⅛ in. short, and insert rear tenons unglued into back stretcher.

Glue front tenons into mortises in front stretcher.

Mortise

Drawer divider

Dovetail pin

building an inner framework, called a *web frame*, to support the drawer or, for a simpler approach, using wooden runners secured to the case, drawer, or aprons of a frame.

Wooden runners work well with both plywood and solid-wood cabinets, as long as you use elongated screw holes when attaching them cross-grain to a solid case to allow the case to expand and contract during the seasons. A traditional web frame is designed with solid-wood cases in mind, permitting case sides and partitions to swell and shrink without affecting the joinery. You'll find this type of construction in most 17th- and 18th-century casework, though it works equally well in modern designs and can still be used in plywood cases.

If there isn't an overhead divider or web frame, attach a strip of wood to the case side above each drawer side to serve as a *kicker* that holds down the back of the drawer to prevent the box from tipping down as it's pulled out. Again, use elongated screw

CASES AND FRAMES FOR DRAWERS

When using metal slides...

FRAMELESS CABINET

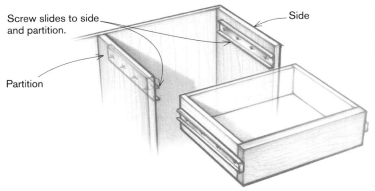

Screw slides to side and partition.

Side

Partition

CABINET WITH FACE FRAME

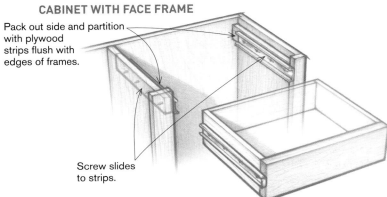

Pack out side and partition with plywood strips flush with edges of frames.

Screw slides to strips.

When using wood-to-wood drawers...

RUNNERS ON CASE

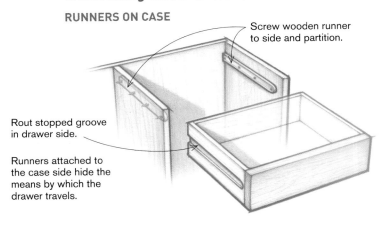

Screw wooden runner to side and partition.

Rout stopped groove in drawer side.

Runners attached to the case side hide the means by which the drawer travels.

RUNNERS ON DRAWER

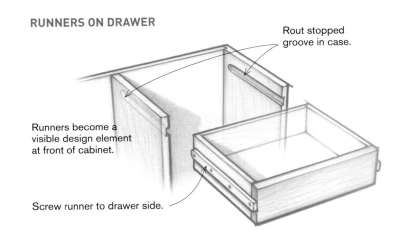

Rout stopped groove in case.

Runners become a visible design element at front of cabinet.

Screw runner to drawer side.

L-SHAPED BLOCKS ON TABLE FRAME

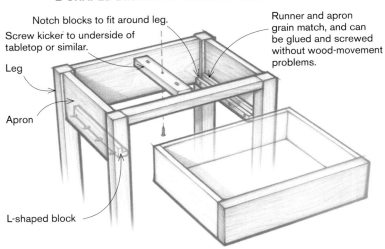

Notch blocks to fit around leg.

Screw kicker to underside of tabletop or similar.

Leg

Apron

L-shaped block

Runner and apron grain match, and can be glued and screwed without wood-movement problems.

WEB FRAME ON SOLID CASE

Gaps at back of frame allow for wood movement.

Kickers prevent drawer from tipping down.

Drawer rides on runners in frame.

holes if screwing the kicker to solid wood case sides. On pieces with interior top frames, such as tables and desks, you can center a single kicker overhead, aligning its lower edge with the top of the drawer opening.

Web frames can include a dust panel in the center, which restrains migrating dust and keeps clothing and other loose items from snagging or catching on an adjacent drawer. Build the panel into the framework as you would any frame-and-panel construction, making it from either plywood or solid wood (see "Door Anatomy," p. 100.).

Drawer Construction

Drawers suffer a lot of joint-straining abuse from yanking them open and slamming them shut, especially when loaded with heavy contents. That's why it's smart to build your drawers so they're as sturdy as possible. And no other area in a drawer is as important as the corner joints. Thankfully, there is no shortage of drawer-joinery options.

As for joining the bottom to the walls, as discussed in Chapter 1 (see "Drawer Anatomy," p. 8), the drawer bottom typically rides in grooves cut in the drawer front and sides. In the case of joints that show from both sides, such as finger joints or through dovetails, you'll have to rout stop grooves to prevent them from showing on the drawer box exterior. If you align the groove with one of the joint elements, you'll only have to stop the grooves in two of the drawer walls, as shown in the right photo below.

The side-to-back joint typically consists of a dado sawn into each side to receive the back. For strength, keep the dado shallow—one-third the thickness of the stock is a good rule of thumb—and pin the joint with nails or staples (see the photos on p. 20). That's not to say that other joints at the back

GROOVING FOR THE BOTTOM. Use a dado blade to mill grooves in the front and sides for the drawer bottom. Grooves are typically ¼ in. wide by ¼ in. (or less) deep, and ¼ in. to ½ in. up from the bottom edge.

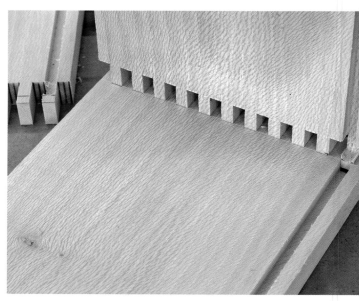

STOP THAT GROOVE. Aligning the drawer bottom groove with one of the joint fingers necessitates stopping the grooves in only two of the drawer walls. The grooves can run through on the mating pieces.

CORNER JOINTS

Rabbet (front) and Dado (back)

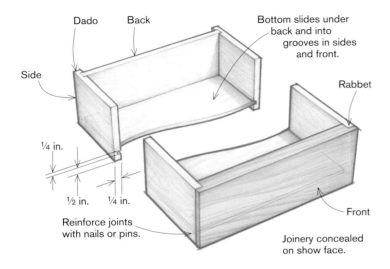

Dado

Back

Side

Bottom slides under back and into grooves in sides and front.

Rabbet

¼ in.

½ in.

¼ in.

Reinforce joints with nails or pins.

Front

Rabbet

Joinery concealed on show face.

Rabbeted Tongue and Dado

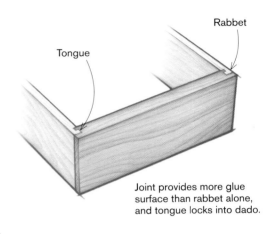

Tongue

Rabbet

Joint provides more glue surface than rabbet alone, and tongue locks into dado.

Through Dovetail

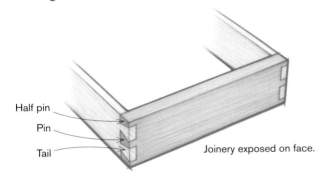

Half pin

Pin

Tail

Joinery exposed on face.

Box Joint

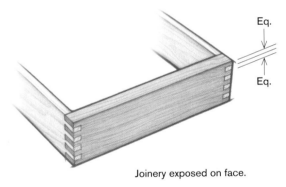

Eq.

Eq.

Joinery exposed on face.

Half-Blind Dovetail

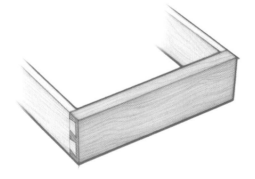

Sliding Dovetail

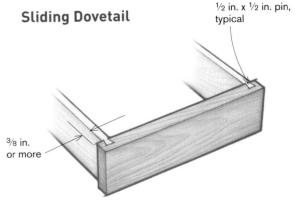

½ in. x ½ in. pin, typical

³⁄₈ in. or more

Front extends past sides for strength.

aren't appropriate, such as box joints or through dovetails, especially in traditional and high-end work.

Typically, the back is narrower than the sides and front, and sits above the drawer bottom groove, with the drawer bottom passing beneath it during assembly. For the front corners, everything else is fair game, ranging from basic rabbet joints to through and half-blind dovetails and other specialty joints, as I'll discuss in a moment.

Choose your joints judiciously. For example, if you're making tall drawers, box joints or dovetails are a good idea to support the load that big drawers hold. Small, diminutive drawers, such as those found in jewelry chests and small boxes, suffer less abuse, so a glued-and-nailed rabbet joint may do. Also, consider your shop's tooling, as well as your experience and production efficiencies. If you lack

machines, a hand-cut joint might be the best route. Or perhaps you have a spare router table that you can dedicate to cutting a specific joint, leaving it set up so that future drawer joints are easier to make.

Dimension your drawer stock before cutting any joints. You can cut the sides to match the full depth of the case (allowing for the joinery at the front), or cut them a bit short and plan to use bumpers or other drawer-stopping hardware (see "Drawer Stops," p. 64). With wood-to-wood drawers, cut the sides and the front to the full height and width of the drawer opening, and plan on shaving the drawer parts down later for a precise fit. Drawers with metal slides sometimes need an extra inch or two of space above the drawer walls to get the drawer in and out. And most slides require a drawer box width that's 1 in. less than the case opening. Be sure to check the manufacturer's instructions.

KEEP IT SHALLOW, AND NAIL IT. Cut a shallow dado in the drawer sides—1/8 in. to 3/16 in. is sufficient in 1/2-in. material—for the side-to-back joint. Glue and pin the joint to reinforce the connection.

work SMART

Smooth all the inside surfaces of your drawer parts before you cut any joints. Otherwise, subsequent planing, scraping, or sanding can compromise the fit of your joints.

RABBET

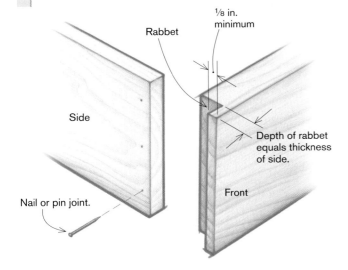

Rabbet

¹⁄₈ in. minimum

Side

Nail or pin joint.

Depth of rabbet equals thickness of side.

Front

RABBETED TONGUE AND DADO

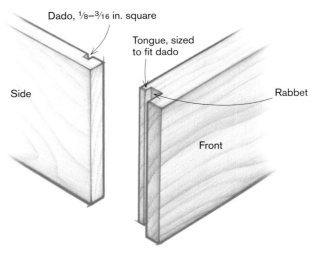

Dado, ¹⁄₈–³⁄₁₆ in. square

Tongue, sized to fit dado

Side

Rabbet

Front

BOX JOINT

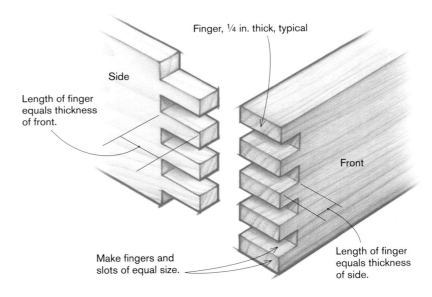

Finger, ¹⁄₄ in. thick, typical

Side

Length of finger equals thickness of front.

Front

Make fingers and slots of equal size.

Length of finger equals thickness of side.

Rabbet, Dado, and Box Joints

A rabbeted drawer is a staple in modern shops. It's relatively strong, quick to make, and looks good because the joinery is concealed at the front of the drawer. A rabbet joint should be reinforced with staples, nails, or pins. If you plan to use a false front on your drawer box, you can hide the fasteners by nailing or stapling through the *front* of the drawer box (see the photos on p. 22). If you choose to nail through the sides, try wooden pins, which add a nice visual element while strengthening the connection.

You can beef up a basic rabbet joint by adding a small tongue in the drawer front and a corresponding dado in the side, making a rabbeted tongue-and-dado joint. Because of the larger gluing area and added mechanical connection, the joint doesn't require pinning.

The box joint, also called a finger joint, has long been used as a corner joint in casework. It works just as well for constructing drawer boxes, which are essentially little cases themselves. The mul-

tiple "fingers" of the joint interlace, making this a particularly strong joint due to the mechanical connection and large gluing area. (For aesthetics, I like to leave a full-width finger at both ends of the joint.) Best of all, cutting the joint is a very simple tablesaw operation and lends itself to production once you set up your saw and build a simple jig.

STAExPLES HIDE BEHIND FRONT. On a false-front drawer, drive staples through the box front and into the sides; this makes a sturdy connection—especially in plywood. The applied front conceals the fasteners.

PINNED WITH BAMBOO. A standard rabbet joint needs extra strength in addition to glue, and it doesn't hurt to beef up a rabbeted tongue-and-dado joint. Adding wooden pins, made from 1/8 in. bamboo skewers, fortifies the joint while adding an attractive touch.

Rabbet

A basic rabbet can be cut in two passes on the tablesaw, as described below. Alternatively, you can cut the rabbet in one pass with a dado blade, feeding the stock flat using the miter gauge with the end of the stock butted against the rip fence. To protect your rip fence, attach a sacrificial face for this operation.

1. Using a standard blade on the tablesaw, first crosscut the inside face with the stock flat on the tablesaw.

2. Rip away the waste by feeding the stock vertically using a tenoning jig.

Rabbeted tongue-and-dado

1. Mill the dado in the side first. Using a standard tablesaw blade, make the dado 1/8 in. to 3/16 in. wide and of equal depth, so it and the corresponding tongue are square in section for strength. **A**

2. Mill the tongue in the front to fit the dado, and cut the rabbet to accept the drawer side. This is easily done by making a series of cuts, standing the work vertically in a tenoning jig. **B** Test-fit the joint, then use clamps when gluing up the drawer box to help squeeze the joints together. Be sure to check for square before setting the box aside to dry.

DADO THE SIDES FIRST. Cut the dado in the sides using a miter gauge and a standard blade. One pass will cut a channel ⅛ in. wide. Move the fence ⅙ in. and make a second cut if you want a slightly wider dado.

RABBET AND TONGUE ARE NEXT. Use a tenoning jig to stand the front upright to saw the rabbet, and then the tongue that fits the dado.

BOX JOINT JIG

A box joint jig is nothing more than a ¾-in.-thick auxiliary plywood fence that you attach to your miter gauge or crosscut sled. Mine is about 6 in. by 18 in. The fence includes a hardwood "pin" that registers each cut from the previous cut.

1. Begin by making the auxiliary fence.

2. To make the pin, rip a short stick of hardwood to the exact thickness of your desired joint pin. Make it a little less wide than the desired length of the finger.

3. Using the same dado blade setup you'll use to cut the workpiece joint, cut a notch in the plywood auxiliary fence, and then glue the pin into the notch.

4. Clamp the jig to the miter gauge or a sled, and use a leftover scrap of the pin stock to align the jig correctly to the blade. Save the scrap pin stock; you'll also use it during the joint-cutting operation.

STICKS ALIGN STOCK. Attach the auxiliary fence, with its registration pin, to your miter gauge or to a crosscut sled. Place a piece of extra pin material between the blade and the pin to align the fence to the blade properly.

A

FIRST CUT AGAINST THE PIN. Cut the first slot in the front or back by butting the stock against the pin, holding the stock vertically.

B

SECOND SLOT IS INDEXED BY FIRST. Simply slip the first slot over the pin to cut the second slot.

C

KEEP ON SLOTTING. Continue cutting all the slots by registering each previous slot on the pin until you reach the opposite edge.

work SMART

Scribing joint shoulders with a marking gauge before cutting is a good technique for joinery work in general, as it leaves a fresh shoulder line and a tight-looking joint.

Box joint

1. Calculate the necessary width of your project stock, taking into account the combined width of all the fingers and notches. Cut the parts to that dimension, or a little wider. If necessary, you can trim the pieces to final width once you've cut the joint.

2. To keep your cuts clean and crisp, it's a good idea to scribe all the shoulders with a marking gauge before making any cuts.

3. Starting with the drawer front piece, stand the part vertically against the fence and butt one edge against the pin to cut the first slot. **A**

4. Slip that slot over the pin to cut the second slot. **B**

5. Continue in this fashion until you've reached the opposite edge. **C**

6. If the mating piece (the drawer side) is thinner than the front, be sure to *raise* the blade equal to the thickness of the front.

7. Orienting the stock so the same edge is facing the pin as it was when you cut the first part, place your scrap pin stock between the jig's pin and the blade to align the stock correctly. **D**

8. Holding the stock firmly, remove the spare pin and make the first shoulder cut. **E**

SHOULDER COMES FIRST. Orient the mating part by placing your scrap pin against the jig's stick and the work. Remove the scrap stick; then make the cut to establish the first shoulder.

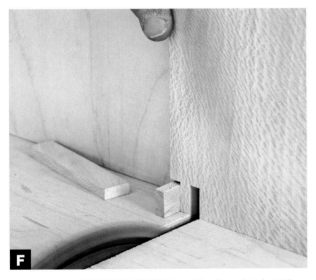

SHOULDER INDEXES THE SLOT. To cut the first slot, butt the shoulder against the pin and push the jig past the blade.

FINISH WITH THE SECOND SHOULDER. As before, continue cutting successive slots until you make the final shoulder cut at the opposite edge.

9. As before, use the previous slot to align the stock to make the next cut. **F**

10. Continue cutting in this manner until you've cut the shoulder at the opposite edge. **G**

11. If you had ripped your workpieces slightly wide, as recommended, you may now need to trim away any excess at the edges so that the joint terminates with full-width fingers and slots.

12. Assemble the joint with glue and clamps—no fasteners are needed. **H**

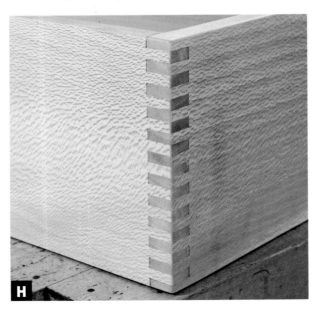

FULL-BODIED FINGERS. The completed joint has full fingers on the top and bottom edges of the drawer front (the part on the right) and requires only glue to keep it together.

Dovetails

Although the dovetail joint can take some esoteric forms, the most common varieties—all found in drawer joinery—are half-blind, through, and sliding.

The half-blind dovetail, also known as a lapped dovetail, is the standard front corner joint for many types of drawers. The joint is concealed at the front, so it's a good choice for projects where you want to hide the joinery from view. As with any type of dovetail, the lapped dovetail is incredibly strong because the angled pins and tails create a wedging effect to lock parts mechanically together. Plus, it looks awesome. The joint can be made with a jig, or by hand.

HALF-BLIND DOVETAIL

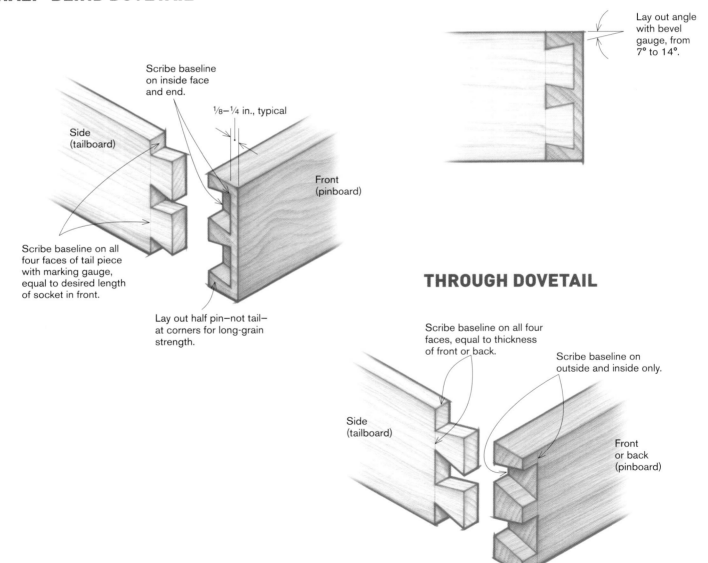

Scribe baseline on inside face and end.

⅛–¼ in., typical

Side (tailboard)

Front (pinboard)

Scribe baseline on all four faces of tail piece with marking gauge, equal to desired length of socket in front.

Lay out half pin—not tail—at corners for long-grain strength.

Lay out angle with bevel gauge, from 7° to 14°.

THROUGH DOVETAIL

Scribe baseline on all four faces, equal to thickness of front or back.

Scribe baseline on outside and inside only.

Side (tailboard)

Front or back (pinboard)

Through dovetails are easier to make than half-blind dovetails. If desired, through dovetails can be used to join drawer sides to the front, with the ends of the tails serving as a decorative element of the drawer front. More common, however, through dovetails are used to join the drawer back to the sides in finely made drawers. Through dovetails can be made with a jig or by hand.

The sliding dovetail, sometimes called a "French dovetail," is a very sturdy joint and is amazingly fast to produce with the right router-table setup. The drawback is that the joint can only be used for drawers with fronts that extend beyond the sides. However, this makes it very handy for drawers with metal slides or other protruding guide systems, because the overhang lets you conceal the runners from the front. A variation is the stopped sliding dovetail, where the joint is concealed and the drawer front extends above the sides as well. This is a useful joint when you need a drawer front that's taller than the sides, such as when there's a horizontal drawer divider in the case above a lipped drawer.

Half-blind dovetail with a jig

One of the easiest methods for cutting half-blind dovetails is to use a commercial dovetail jig and a router equipped with a guide bushing and dovetail bit. Many jigs can cut both half-blind as well as through dovetails. In use, the drawer sides clamp vertically to the front of the jig, while the drawer front and back are clamped horizontally to its top. When routing half-blind dovetails, the tails and their sockets are cut at the same time, as the bushing in the router follows a metal template secured to the jig. Every jig comes with complete instructions, but I'll summarize the process here.

SLIDING DOVETAIL

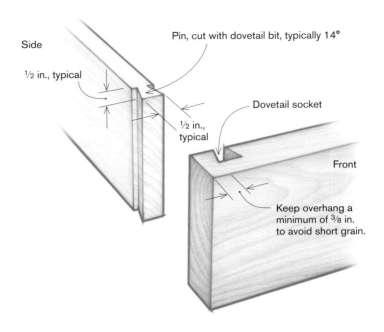

Side

½ in., typical

Pin, cut with dovetail bit, typically 14°

Dovetail socket

½ in., typical

Front

Keep overhang a minimum of ⅜ in. to avoid short grain.

STOPPED SLIDING DOVETAIL

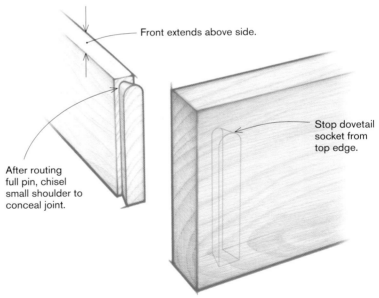

Front extends above side.

After routing full pin, chisel small shoulder to conceal joint.

Stop dovetail socket from top edge.

A

B

SET THE STOPS. Stops at each end of the dovetail jig locate the stock for proper placement. Shop-made notes on both stops signify left, right, front, and back ends of the drawer side, drawer front and back, lessening the chance of mistakes.

GUIDING FINGERS. A guide bushing in the router follows the fingers of a metal template, cutting the half-blind dovetails and their sockets at the same time.

1. Set the stops on the jig to locate the front and back pieces. One trick for avoiding confusion is to mark the jig for the left, right, front, and back edges of the drawer parts. **A**

2. Outfit your router with the guide bushing and dovetail bit that came with your jig. Adjust the bit projection as per the jig's instructions.

work SMART

It's best to design your drawer heights to suit the spacing of the jig's template fingers. This is especially true if, for example, you want to begin and end your joint with a half-pin, which is the most sound construction for a dovetail joint, or if you want to make sure that there is enough space below the bottom groove for strength.

3. With the drawer parts mounted in the jig and the router bit adjusted as explained in the jig's instructions, rout the tails and pins. **B**

4. After routing the pins and tails, locate the groove for the drawer bottom so it falls in the center of a tail, thus concealing it from view. Saw the groove on the tablesaw.

5. Glue up the drawer box. A light sanding is all you should need to clean up the sides and make the joint flush. **C**

TIGHT AND STURDY. The glued and assembled joint needs only a light swipe from a plane or some sanding before being put into service.

REMOVING GLUE

Using too much glue during assembly is wasteful and causes a mess on your work, your bench, and you. Even careful application results in glue squeezing out of joints when they're assembled, so it's smart to remove this stuff before a finish is applied or it will show up as a glaring smear under the finish. You can wait until the glue is semi-dry, and then peel it up with a chisel, but I prefer to tackle the mess as it occurs, using a damp—not wet—rag and a sharp chisel.

WIPE, SCRAPE, AND WIPE AGAIN. Rub the surface with a damp rag, refolding it continually to expose a clean area. While the surface is still wet, use a sharp chisel in a pulling action to scrape away remaining glue. Finish up with a few more swipes from the rag.

BANDSAW KEEPS CUTS SQUARE. Start with the tails first, sawing as straight as possible along each angle up to the baseline. If your blade is square to the table, the dovetail cheeks will be square to the face of the stock.

Half-blind and through-dovetail by hand

Hallmarks of fine work, the half-blind and through-dovetail joints have been used for centuries in fine furniture, and both continue to be a standard by which modern drawer joints are judged. Although each can be cut using a jig, making this joint by hand offers a chance to hone your hand-tool skills and imparts a visible sense of finely crafted woodworking. I typically employ hand-cut versions of these joints on my best work.

To make the joint, I usually cut the tails first, then mark out the pins from them. "Pins-first" woodworkers do it the other way around. Either method works. I'll explain the "tails-first" method here.

1. Scribe a baseline around the joint areas using a marking gauge, adjusting the gauge to the thickness of the stock and, in the case of half-blind dovetails, to the desired length of the tails.

2. Lay out the spacing and slope for the tails with a pencil and bevel gauge, making the angle anywhere from 7 degrees to 14 degrees (your aesthetic choice) for strength.

3. Traditionalists cut the tails with a backsaw, but I "cheat" a bit by using the bandsaw, which I find to be faster and more accurate, even for beginners. Simply bandsaw each angle right to the baseline, making the cut as straight as you can. **A** Nibble away the waste as much as possible, staying just a bit away from the baseline.

4. Use a chisel to chop and pare away the remaining waste right to the scribe line, undercutting slightly inward from each face.

5. Use the tails to lay out the pins on the drawer back or front (called the *pinboard*). Clamp the

DRAW THE PINS. Holding the stock firmly, use a long pointed knife to follow the outline of the tails as you mark the pinboard.

ANGLED ON THE FRONT. Cut the half-blind pins on the drawer front by clamping the work-piece vertically in the vise and making an angled cut to the baselines on the inside face and the end.

pinboard vertically in the vise, with its upper end aligned with a piece of scrap placed under the tailboard. Align the edges of the two drawer parts by holding a straight stick against them. If you're making through-dovetails, slide the tailboard forward along the stick until its inside baseline aligns with the inside face of the pinboard. If you're making lapped dovetails, align the end of the tailboard with the scribed baseline on the end of the pinboard.

6. Press down on the work, and scribe around each tail and onto the pin board with a pointed blade, such as a craft knife. **B**

7. Use a fine-toothed backsaw to saw the cheeks of the half-blind pins on the front, making a sloping cut that extends between your scribed lines. **C**

8. Cut the cheeks of the through-pins on the drawer back and saw straight across for the full pins. **D**

STRAIGHT ACROSS FOR THE BACK. The through-pins on the drawer back are cut with the saw held perpendicular to the end of the workpiece. Keep sawing until the blade reaches the baseline on both sides.

DEFINE THE SHOULDER FIRST. Make a very light paring cut to the baseline to establish the shoulder, prying up the waste gently with the chisel.

9. Chisel out the waste. Clamp the work securely on the bench, and start with a single, very light cut, beginning at the center of the waste area and paring inward from the end of the workpiece to the baseline. **E**

10. Follow with a series of alternating cuts to remove the waste, chopping downward at the baseline **F**, and then tapping inward from the end.

11. Complete the half-blind pins by clamping the work vertically and paring lightly to the baseline and to the uncut, inside corners. **G** Use a narrow chisel to trim the end-grain surface in the corners.

12. With the through-pinboard, flip the stock over after you've chopped halfway through, and use the same chopping and tapping procedure until the bulk of the waste is removed. **H**

13. Use a narrow chisel to pare away any remaining fibers at the baseline of the pins.

14. Dry-fit the joint by gently tapping all the parts together to see if any area needs fine-tuning with a chisel. Just as gently, take the joint apart, being careful not to split any fibers. If all the joints seat fully onto their respective baselines, you're ready to glue and assemble.

CUTTING DOWN BEFORE TAPPING IN. Chop directly downward at the baseline, taking relatively light cuts before chopping inward from the end to remove the waste.

PARE INTO THE CORNERS. Because the handsaw didn't reach into the corners, finish up the half-blind pins by paring to the baseline and the inside corners by hand.

CHOP THE OTHER SIDE. Once you chop halfway into the through-pinboard, flip it over and remove the waste by chopping from the opposite face. Afterward, clean up any excess with a narrow chisel.

SOCKET FIRST. With the bit height set to the desired pin length, rout the sockets in the front first. A wide backup piece helps steer the work and limits tear-out at the back.

ONE SETUP CUTS THE PIN. Feeding the workpiece with a wide backup board, rout the pin using the same bit and bit height used for the socket. After routing one side, flip the stock and rout the opposite side.

Sliding dovetail with a router

The key to cutting the sliding dovetail is to use the same dovetail bit for the dovetail socket and the pin.

1. Rout the socket, guiding the workpiece against the fence and backing it up with a wide board to prevent cocking the work as it moves past the bit. **A** On hard or tough woods, you can reduce stress to the bit and the work by cutting a dado in the work on the tablesaw prior to routing the socket.

2. Without changing the height of the bit, move the fence toward the bit and set up the cut for the pin. Rout one side of the pin by standing the work vertically, using a wide guide block, and feeding slowly as the bit exits to reduce blowout at the back.

C

D

TAP IT HOME. Because there's so much surface area, you'll need to tap the joint home with a hammer. Using contrasting woods makes the joint really stand out.

3. Flip the work over and repeat the cut to rout the opposite side, producing a full pin. **B**

4. Assemble the joint with glue, driving the tailboard home with firm taps from a mallet or hammer. The glue will help seat the joint and keep it from shifting. **C** If you use contrasting woods for the side and front, the joint really pops when a finish is applied. **D**

Drawer Assembly

Most drawers can be assembled easily with some glue, a few clamps, and perhaps a few nails or staples. Your primary concern is that the drawer box goes together flat and square in order to simplify subsequent fitting to the case. For most joints, I apply glue with a typical glue brush (also sold as a

solder flux brush), which provides good control. It's important to have all your supplies on hand so you can work quickly to assemble the joint before the glue sets.

Part of the assembly process includes adding the drawer bottom. You have several choices for your drawer bottoms, as I'll discuss in a few moments.

Assembling dovetails

Dovetail joints can be fussy to glue up, so following the correct assembly steps is important for success.

1. Starting with the inside face, brush a dab of glue on the tails and along the edges of each pin opening on the tailboards. Also coat the end-grain surfaces of half-blind tails.

FULL COVERAGE. Use a small brush to apply an even, thin coat of glue to all inside mating joint surfaces on the tailboards and pinboards.

CLOSE THE BOX. Attach the drawer back to the side in the same manner as the front, then tap the remaining side down onto the front and back. A fist should provide enough pressure, but keep clamps on hand, just in case.

work SMART

It's wise to use white glue for assembling dovetails, as it provides more "open assembly time" than yellow glue, giving you more time to get the joint together before the glue starts setting up.

2. Apply glue to the pinboards, coating the inside faces and both cheeks of the pins and their adjacent baseline areas. **A**

3. With all the joints wet with glue, connect the drawer front to one side by pushing the joint together by hand.

4. Add the back to the assembly, and then close the box by tapping the remaining side onto both the back and front. **B**

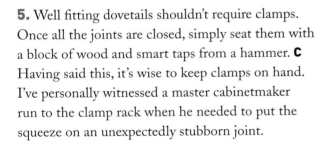

TAPPING, NOT CLAMPING. Seat the joint by tapping on a wedge-shaped block positioned over every tail.

PINCH IT SQUARE. Use a pinch rod to check for square, comparing opposing diagonals and adjusting the shape of the drawer until the distances are equal. Measure all the way to the bottom of a tall drawer to check for twist.

5. Well fitting dovetails shouldn't require clamps. Once all the joints are closed, simply seat them with a block of wood and smart taps from a hammer. **C** Having said this, it's wise to keep clamps on hand. I've personally witnessed a master cabinetmaker run to the clamp rack when he needed to put the squeeze on an unexpectedly stubborn joint.

6. Check the box for square before setting it aside to dry. When doing this, work on a truly flat surface, or you won't get an accurate measurement. You can check for square by comparing opposing diagonal dimensions with a tape measure, tapping or pushing the box into shape until the diagonals match. However, a more accurate method, especially with tall drawers, is to use a pinch rod instead of a tape measure, checking at various points inside the box. **D**

7. If the drawer rocks on your flat surface, it means it's twisted. If the twist isn't too bad, you can often flatten it by placing some weight on top as the glue dries. But don't try to force it by using anything too heavy; a No. 5 or No. 6 hand plane should work fine. When the drawer checks out square and flat, set it aside on a truly flat surface until the glue has dried.

FIXING GAPS

Perfection in woodworking is a goal, but seldom a reality. Even the best among us encounter gaps in joints now and then. To fix them, you can use a variety of techniques. Cyanoacrylate glue ("super glue") comes in various viscosities, and can mask small cracks with aplomb. Spread some of the thick variety stuff into the crack, and immediately rub it into the joint with some sandpaper or a few hand-plane shavings. It will harden in seconds, at which point you can sand the dried glue smooth. If necessary, repeat this process a few times until the gaps are filled and level. Subsequent sanding with finer sandpaper and a coat of finish over the area will hide the repair. If the gap is more substantial, you can glue a small wedge into the opening. Let the glue dry, pare the wedge flush with a chisel, and sand it smooth. No one will see your "flaw."

Another approach is to wait until you've applied the final coat of finish to the piece, including the problem area. After the last coat dries, fill any gaps by rubbing over them with moderate pressure using a colored wax crayon. These crayons come in just about every wood color imaginable, and are available wherever you buy finishing supplies. Finish by buffing the area with a soft cloth to remove the excess wax.

SAVED BY SUPERGLUE. Cyanoacrylate glue works well to fill small cracks. Squeeze it into the gaps, then quickly rub the area with fine wood shavings or sand it with fine-grit paper to force the wood dust into the glue.

WEDGE IT CLOSED. For larger gaps, try gluing a small wedge made from the same wood into the crack. Once the glue has set, trim it flush and no one will be the wiser.

BOTTOM BEVELS. Bevel the edges of a drawer bottom by angling the blade about 15° and guiding the panel against a tall fence. If you plan to slide the bottom under the drawer back, bevel only the two sides and the front edge.

Adding the bottom

For a high-end "feel" to your work, you can make drawer bottoms from solid wood, as was done traditionally. However, that may require edge-joining boards to make wider panels. Many woodworkers prefer to use plywood instead, because it's available in large panels.

A drawer bottom can be the same thickness as the width of the drawer groove, or you can rabbet or bevel the edges of a thicker panel to fit. On medium-sized drawers, I advise using thicker bottoms. Although a ¼-in.-thick bottom will certainly work, the tinny "clack" it emits when objects hit the drawer tends to humble the project. For higher-end drawers, try beefing up your bottoms by using more rigid ⅜-in.- or ½-in.-thick plywood or solid wood instead.

Rather than widening a typical ¼-in.-wide groove to accommodate a thicker drawer bottom, it's better to bevel or rabbet the edges of the bottom

to fit the groove. The traditional method is to bevel the edges of a solid-wood bottom, orienting the tapers toward the underside of the drawer. (This works for plywood, too.) The tablesaw makes quick work of this. Use a scrap piece to set up the cut, adjusting the fence until the beveled edge fits into the groove. And remember: If you use solid wood, orient the grain direction from side to side. (see "Drawer Anatomy," p. 8.)

Another option is to bevel the edges on the router table or shaper using a panel-raising bit to cut the profile of your choosing. Or, you can rabbet the edges on the tablesaw to create a tongue of the appropriate size. Typically, the tongue is made as thick as the drawer groove width, but a tad longer than the groove's depth. The rabbet is typically oriented to the underside of the drawer so the inside of the box remains a clean, uninterrupted surface.

Outfitting your drawer with a removable bottom is a standard practice in the trade and a good idea

RABBETED TO SLIDE UNDERNEATH. A rabbet cut into the edges of the drawer bottom creates a tongue that slides into the grooves in the drawer sides.

SQUARE BEFORE NAILING. Once the bottom is in place, check for square by measuring opposite corners. Then secure the bottom to the back with nails or staples.

should you ever need to repair or replace it. The key here is to cut the drawer back narrower than the sides so you can slide the bottom under the drawer back and into its grooves in the sides and front. Nails or screws that secure the bottom to the back can be easily removed should the need arise.

Another advantage to a drawer bottom that slides in like this is that it affords you one last chance to square up the drawer, which is critical to its proper operation. Make sure to cut the bottom square and, after inserting it, check the drawer for square before fastening the bottom to the drawer back.

Using a plywood bottom affords one unique advantage over solid wood: there's no wood movement to worry about. Therefore, if you like, you can glue the bottom into its grooves, adding significant strength to the drawer's corner joints. Just remember that future repairs will be difficult or impossible, so reserve the technique for large utility drawers and monster-size boxes that really need the additional strength. In fact, if you plan to glue in a bottom, it's smart to "capture" it all the way around, making the drawer back the same height as the sides, and grooving it as well. In that case, you'll assemble the entire drawer in one shot.

PLYWOOD CAN BE GLUED. For a super-strong drawer, cut the back to full height and groove it, then glue a plywood bottom into all the grooves, assembling the entire drawer in one step.

3 FITTING AND FINISHING DRAWERS

Fitting a drawer box to its case is one of the keys to a sweet-running drawer. Sometimes this calls for removing just a whisper of wood on the drawer sides for the perfect fit, and checking that there's enough room above the drawer for seasonal expansion. It's a good idea to keep your planes and scrapers razor sharp, then use them to fine-tune the final fit. If you're using metal slides, installation will be a breeze because no final fitting is necessary.

One exciting aspect of drawer making is choosing the right pull for the job. There are literally thousands of choices, ranging from shop-made pulls to commercial knobs and handles made from assorted materials in an endless array of styles. From traditional to contemporary, there's sure to be a pull that's perfect for your project.

Let's not forget to consider how our drawers will come to a stop inside the case. It's usually best to provide some sort of cushioning effect so a drawer won't slam shut with a *thunk*. Stops and bumpers come into play here, as do locks and catches. You should also consider whether you want to limit how far a drawer can be pulled out of the case, so you can avoid accidents and keep drawer contents from spilling onto the floor. And to keep your drawers gliding with ease over the long term, proper lubrication of key drawer parts is a step not to be missed.

Installing Metal Slides

If you're using metal slides, and if you sized your drawer parts carefully, most of the hard work is behind you. Standard side- or corner-mount slides are straightforward to install. You need to deduct the required space for the slides from the case opening, then build the drawer to that dimension. Most slides require a total of 1 in. of space, or ½ in. on each side of the drawer, so drawers are typically 1 in. less than the width of the opening. The math is simple, and most slides allow drawers to be oversized or undersized by as much as 1/16 in., which is nice insurance if your assembled drawer turns out a bit wider or narrower than planned.

If you end up with a drawer that's too wide or too narrow, most fixes are simple. Narrow drawers can be shimmed to fit by adding slips of veneer between the slides and the case. If a solid-wood drawer is too wide, plane or sand the sides evenly until the box fits the opening. If a drawer with plywood sides is only a bit too wide, remove one or both slides from the drawer sides and saw a wide, shallow groove to remount the slide. If the drawer is substantially oversized, cut away or knock apart one side, recut the front and back to proper length, then recut and assemble the joints. Of course, a final option is simply to build another drawer.

Side-mount slides

1. Install the runners on the drawer so they're parallel with its bottom or top edge, and at a height relative to the desired drawer height in the case. Position the front end of each runner even with, or slightly set back from, the front of the drawer. (Check the instructions that come with the slides.)

2. Attach the slide housings into the case, using the same procedure as you would for undermount slides, beginning with step 4, as discussed below.

A

INSTALL, THEN MEASURE. Install undermount slides into the case, then measure the outside-to-outside distance between the moveable parts of the slides. Make your drawer width to that dimension plus the combined thickness of its sides.

Undermount slides

With undermount slides, the drawer-half of each slide tucks in underneath the drawer, resting against the drawer bottom and the inside face of each drawer side. These slides—especially the newer variety with the self-close feature—are easy to install, but require a slightly different approach when it comes to dimensioning the drawer.

1. Install the slides into the case to get a measurement for the drawer's width. **A**

2. After building the drawer to fit the space between the slides, screw to the underside the two clips that connect to the slides as the drawer is pushed in. **B & C**

3. Each slide also has a small metal hook that grasps the back of the drawer to prevent it from tipping under load when extended. Drill small holes or add a wooden ledger at the back of the drawer to engage the hook. **D & E**

4. Install the case-mounted half of each slide. If the cabinet has an overhanging face frame, shim out the slides by attaching spacers to the case sides and partitions. On a cabinet with horizontal dividers, position the slides level with the dividers. **F**

B

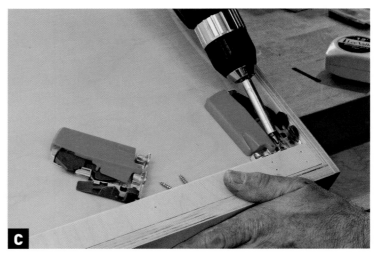

C

ATTACH THE LATCH. Clips screwed to the bottom front of the drawer engage the slides when the drawer is pushed into its opening. To release, simply squeeze the clips and pull the drawer out.

If your cabinet has no horizontal dividers, begin installation with the topmost pair of slides, and cut a plywood spacer to support them at the desired height. Once the first pair is in place, cut down the spacer for the next pair, and so on, until you've installed the bottom-most slides. **G** This method guarantees your slides are evenly spaced and square to the case, which ensures your drawers are as well.

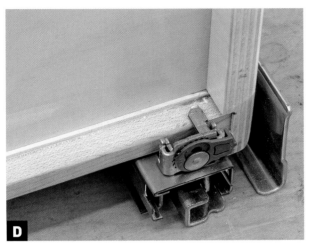

D

STRIP PREVENTS TIP. To prevent the drawer from tipping down, nail a ledger strip to the back of the drawer to give grab to a metal hook at the back of the slide when installing the drawer.

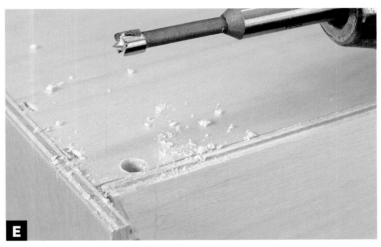

E

A HOLE WORKS, TOO. Another method of securing the drawer is to drill a small hole into the drawer back just above the bottom, to engage the slide's hook. Use a Forstner bit to avoid drilling through.

F

SHIM AND LEVEL. For divided cases with overhanging face frames, glue and nail plywood spacers to the case sides and to any partitions to bring the slides even with the drawer openings, and install the slides level with the dividers.

PLACE IT WITH A SPACER. In undivided cases, install the uppermost pair of slides first, using a plywood spacer to ensure the pair are of equal height and square to the case. Install the remaining slides by cutting the spacer down in successive increments.

G

Fitting False Drawer Fronts

Attaching a false front to a drawer is a good way to dress up what would otherwise be a rather ordinary box. And it's a good choice if you're attaching slides to the sides of the drawer because it can conceal the hardware. It's also an easy way to create an overlay drawer, because the joinery is simplified: You just build a drawer box with your choice of corner joints, then attach an overhanging front to the box. Or perhaps you want to make a down 'n dirty drawer box (such as a plywood box with stapled rabbet joints), and hide the joinery by adding a showy piece of wood for the front. Whichever the case, make sure to allow for the extra thickness of the false front when dimensioning the depth of the drawer box.

Fitting false fronts is best done once the drawer boxes are installed in the case. With the drawer in place, you simply cut the front to size and attach it to the installed box with screws driven through the box, so no hardware is seen on the face of the drawer. Make sure to dimension the front so it has room to expand upward, particularly on extra-tall drawers (see "Fitting a Wood-to-Wood Drawer," p. 50).

Attaching an interior drawer front

It's easiest to attach a false front to an interior pull-out or other type of drawer that's not tightly adjacent to another one.

1. On the inside of the drawer front, use a drill/countersink bit to drill countersunk holes for screws. **A**

2. Secure the positioned drawer front with clamps, and drive the screws into the back of the front from inside the box. **B**

Attaching a column of drawer fronts

Typically, false drawer fronts are attached to the "public" face of a case. One of the more challenging situations is attaching false fronts to a column of inset drawers or to drawers that are separated by dividers. However, the fitting process is greatly simplified if you follow a few logical steps.

1. Beginning with the lowest drawer, position its false front by placing a couple of shims at the bottom of the opening to create the desired reveal, then clamp the front to the box. **C**

SINK FROM BEHIND. Using a drill/countersink bit, bore through the box front to drill holes for screws.

CLAMP AND SCREW. Clamp the front in position and screw it to the drawer box from inside the drawer.

SCREW IT TWICE. Pull out the drawer and drive two screws through countersunk holes in the drawer box and into the front. Close the drawer and check the reveals, then drive the remaining screws.

SHIM, THEN CLAMP. Slide a couple of shims under the drawer front to create the desired gap at the bottom, and then clamp the front to the drawer box.

2. Pull out the drawer, and screw the front on from behind, using only two screws at opposite corners at first. **D**

3. Close the drawer and check the reveal. If it's consistent, drill holes for the remaining screws and install them. If not, remove the first pair of screws, adjust the fit, and install the remaining screws. Finish up by adding the first pair of screws.

4. With the bottom-most drawer front in place, use the shims to position the drawer front directly above it, again clamping the front to the box and securing it with screws from the inside. **E**

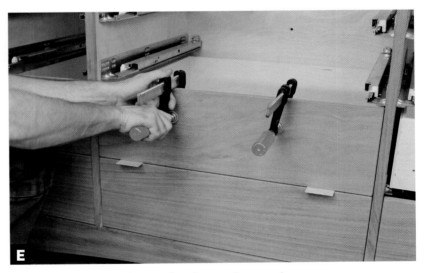

SPACE FOR CLAMPS. As long as there's enough space above, you can clamp each successive drawer front in place, moving upward.

TAPE INSTEAD OF CLAMPS. When there's no way to clamp a drawer front in place, use squares of double-sided tape instead to secure the front for screwing.

LOOKS GOOD OUTSIDE. The completed drawer front is clean on the outside, hiding all the drawer-front screws and drawer-pull hardware inside.

TEMPORARY PULLS

Fitting a drawer typically involves inserting and removing it frequently. While it would be convenient to mount the actual drawer pull at this point, it could get in the way of your work. A screw serves as a great temporary pull. Drive it into the front so it corresponds to the future pull's location. The screw is easily removed and replaced any number of times, and the screw hole will eventually be covered by the permanent pull, letting you continue the fitting process with a surefire method of getting the drawer out of the case.

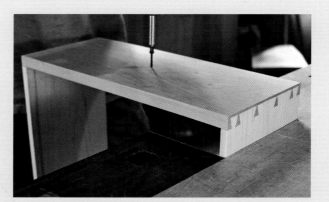

PROVISIONAL PULL. A screw driven into the front at the spot where the drawer's permanent pull will be located offers a means to get the drawer out of the case during the fitting stage.

5. Things get tricky when you get to a top drawer that doesn't allow clamping access due to a top or divider in the way. Here, it's best to use double-sided tape attached to the front of the drawer box, again using shims to create the bottom gap, then pressing the false front onto the box. **F**

6. With the front taped in position, gently pull out the drawer, apply clamps for reinforcement, and attach the front with screws from behind as before, again using the two-screw method in case the front shifts a bit during the process. The result is a clean-looking drawer with all the attachment hardware hidden inside the box. **G**

Sizing Wooden Runners

To maximize useable space inside a cabinet, make your drawers as large as possible by using wooden runners attached to the case sides. The runners fit into stopped grooves cut in the drawer sides, allowing you to hang drawers directly above and below each other without losing space to drawer dividers in the case. The drawer is stopped when the ends of the runners contact the stopped groove in the drawer. Fitting a drawer with wooden runners is simple because you can plane or sand the runners to an exact fit in the drawer grooves *before* installing them, ensuring the drawer will ride smoothly.

In general, it's best to size the drawer about ⅛ in. less in width than the drawer opening. If door hinges or other hardware gets in the way, make the drawer narrower to clear these obstructions, then make your runners thicker.

1. Rout a ³⁄₁₆-in. deep stopped groove in each drawer side. **A**

2. Mill the runners oversized in length, making them slightly wider than your drawer groove and a bit thicker than the depth of the groove plus the required space between the drawer and the case.

A

STOP THAT GROOVE. Using the router table, rout a stopped groove in each side of the drawer. Lower the work onto a spinning straight bit, with scrap clamped to the table to stop the groove at the desired point.

B

EASY TO FIT. Hand-plane the edges of each runner until it slides freely but without play in the groove. Bandsaw or sand an arc on one end to match the curved end of the groove.

Use a hand plane or a carefully controlled sander to trim and smooth the edges of each runner until it just slides in the drawer groove. **B**

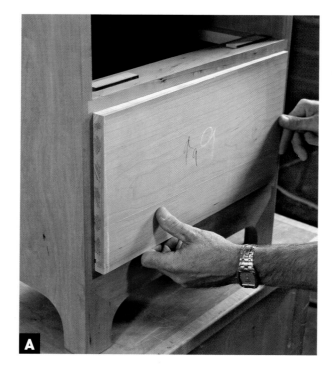

RUN IT STRAIGHT. Place a spacer under the runner to align it parallel with the case and with its twin runner. Screw it to the case through countersunk holes that slightly recess the screw heads.

FIT BEFORE YOU BUILD. Before cutting the drawer joints, size the front to the exact dimensions of the drawer opening, even if the opening is cocked slightly or out of square.

3. Once the runners slide freely, round the front end of each to match the end of the stopped groove in the drawer. Then calculate the runners' length to stop the drawer at the desired location, and cut the runner to finished length.

4. Install the runners in the case with screws. **C**

5. The drawer shouldn't quite fit onto the runners at this point because they should still be a bit too thick. Note how much wood needs to be removed from the face of the runners, remove them from the case, and use a plane to shave them down slightly thinner. Then reinstall them to check the fit. You're done fitting when the drawer barely rubs the faces of both runners and glides in and out of the case, at which point you can remount the runners permanently with glue.

Fitting a Wood-to-Wood Drawer

Woodworkers refer to a drawer fitted super-close to its opening as a "piston fit" drawer. That's what we're after when fitting a wood-to-wood drawer. It should track as if on rails—smooth and sure. A piston-fit drawer slows a bit at the end of its inward travel as it pushes against a cushion of trapped air. It's remarkable to feel in the hand, and it's a drawer-making technique worth learning.

The fit depends upon the proper amount of space between the drawer sides and the case sides or partitions. In this case, less is more. Like a piston in its cylinder, smooth action depends on a small, but precise gap that won't allow the drawer box to rack in the opening. But there's more than just the width of the drawer to consider. The height is critical, too, and must allow for wood movement. If the drawer wall is too tall, it will bind in its opening as it swells during humid weather. On the other hand, a too-short wall will shrink in height during dry weather, causing the drawer to tip and possibly bind as it's pulled out. The correct gap, or *reveal*, between the top of the drawer and the case parts, is critical to smooth operation.

Narrow drawers allow a smaller gap between the top of the drawer and the case opening. Bigger drawers need more allowance because wide wood expands more. Generally, allow up to 1/16 in. wood movement for drawers 4 in. or less in height, and about 1/8 in. for drawers up to 10 in. tall. Of course, this is just a guide; the particular season in which you fit the drawer (dry or wet, or in between), the type of wood you use and its specific cut (quartersawn versus plainsawn, for example) are all factors that help determine how much gap you need to leave.

1. Fitting a wood drawer actually begins with building it to the proper dimensions. Size the drawer front so it's the exact size of the drawer opening—even if your opening is slightly out of square or irregular. It should almost fit into the case, but not quite. **A** Then dimension the rest of the drawer parts using the front as a guide, and build the drawer. If all goes well, the drawer will match the opening precisely, and will need to be shaved down in small amounts before it can enter the opening.

2. Once the drawer is assembled, check it for twist by placing it bottom-side down on a flat surface such as your tablesaw or a *flat* bench. **B**

3. Remove all twist and level the bottom of the drawer by clamping it upside down on the bench and trimming the high spots with a plane. **C**

ROCK THE BOTTOM. Check for twist in the drawer box by placing it bottom-side down on a flat surface and noting which, if any, corners rock. The corners that don't rock are the high spots.

HIT THE HIGH SPOTS. Turn the drawer upside down and plane the high spots to level the bottom of the drawer.

PLANE AROUND. Plane the top of the drawer as you did the bottom, aiming for the appropriate gap between drawer and case. Swing the plane around the corners to prevent grain tear-out.

4. Plane the top of the drawer level, allowing enough room for seasonal expansion and contraction. To fit the drawer, plane all four edges, keeping the surface smooth and consistent by pivoting the plane around the corners and taking an even amount from each edge. **D**

5. Plane a few chamfers on the drawer box, beveling the bottom corners of the sides at the rear to ease entry into the case, and easing the back corners to prepare the drawer for the next step. **E & F**

6. Having sized the drawer to fit its opening exactly, it shouldn't slide in quite yet. Secure the work to the bench and shave each side of the drawer, planing from front to back to avoid tearing the joints at the front. The chamfer you cut at the back prevents blowout as the plane exits. **G** There is a great deal of back-and-forth in this process, taking a few shavings and then offering the drawer up to its opening to check your progress, and then planing again.

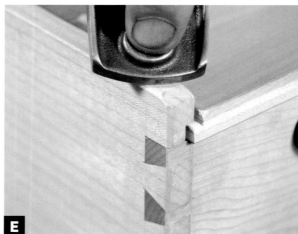

EASE THE EDGES. Plane a ramp on the bottom of the sides at the back to ease the drawer's entry into the case, and chamfer the back corners to prevent tear-out when planing the sides.

PLANE TO FIT. Take a series of light shavings, moving the plane across the drawer side in successive passes to keep the surface flat. Offer the drawer up to the case frequently to check the fit.

FIXING UNSIGHTLY REVEALS

Whoa! You planed off too much wood, and now your drawer has a big ugly gap at the top. Relax, it's a common mistake and easy to fix. First, plane the bottom edges of the drawer (front and two sides, or all four it you have a back that's of equal height). Make the surface straight and level, and the edges sharp and crisp. In other words, joint the edges.

Next, rip some strips of wood slightly thicker than your desired gap, selecting stock that best matches the color and grain of the drawer, especially the front. Glue and clamp the strips to the jointed edges, working on a bench or other stout, flat surface, and using cauls to distribute clamp pressure. Once the glue has dried, level and smooth the strips with a plane, this time being a bit more vigilant when fitting the drawer.

FIRST, MAKE IT EVEN SMALLER. To conceal the glue lines, joint the bottom edges until the corners are sharp to the touch. Take equal amounts off all three edges, keeping the surface flat and of consistent height.

ADD A NEW BOTTOM. Glue and clamp the strips to the bottom of the drawer, using a tall wood caul for the front strip and a thick panel for the side strips.

LESS IS BEST. Aim for 1/64 in. or less of space between the side and the case for a smooth-running drawer. Any bigger, and the drawer may rack and bind as it slides.

THE CORRECT FIT. With almost no gap between sides and case, a small reveal at the bottom, and enough room at the top for wood expansion, this drawer is ready for years of faithful service.

MARKING YOUR DRAWERS

Keeping track of parts as you build is always a good idea, including marking completed work. Drawers that are custom-fit to their respective openings shouldn't be overlooked, since they'll likely enter an opening of similar size but not fit as intended. Once you've fitted a drawer, be sure to mark it permanently, and perhaps its specific case opening in the case as well. Not only will the mark help you keep track of the drawer as you work it, but future owners will thank you for helping them keep their drawers in order.

TRACK WHERE IT GOES. The back of a drawer is an inconspicuous spot to note where a specific drawer resides. Scribe the mark with a knife or use a permanent pen.

7. When the drawer slides the full depth of the case without binding, sand or scrape the sides as smooth and flat as possible. You've fit the drawer when it slides in and out freely, but with no more than 1/64 in. of play from side to side. Less is even better. **H**

8. Cut down and bevel the underside of the front. This prevents the front from catching as it's pushed into the case and it's also your chance to create an even gap at the bottom. Take a few shavings from the bottom edge, beveling the surface toward the back of the drawer front by eye and removing enough wood to leave a small, consistent reveal at the face. The final fit should leave consistent, hairline gaps along the sides, a small reveal at the bottom, and the appropriate gap at the top, including the tops of the sides and back when they're deep in the case. **I**

Leveling Inset Drawer Fronts

The fronts of inset drawers typically need to be trimmed flush to the case front after being fit into their openings. Even if you made your drawers the correct depth, Murphy's Law dictates that the drawer fronts won't align perfectly with the front of the case, requiring some touch-up work. Luckily, there are several methods for truing the faces.

Planing one drawer at a time

The simplest approach is to sand or plane each drawer front individually, gauging the amount of protrusion with one of the most sensitive and accurate tools in the shop: your fingertip.

1. Note the amount and location of any proud areas, then clamp the drawer in the bench, and plane the face. **A** Alternatively, you can hang the drawer on a stout board cantilevered off your bench. **B** Plane a bit, then check the fit. Keep planing and checking in this manner until the drawer face sits level with the face of the case.

2. Give the front a light sanding to smooth and flatten the surface.

work SMART

While it's possible to get very good results leveling drawer fronts with a power sander, there's always the danger of rounding the edges or creating dips in the surface. Also, it's hard to gauge how much material you've removed. A hand plane won't create dips, and your pile of shavings helps indicate how much wood you're removing. If you do use a belt sander, try mounting a sanding frame to the tool. Sanding frames are available for many common sanders, and offer a broader and more stable footprint to prevent tipping and gouging the work.

SHAVE WITH PRECISION. After noting where the drawer front extends past the case, set the plane for a light cut, and work those areas only.

HANG IT OUT. A good way to support a drawer for working it is to mount it over a thick, wide board clamped to the bench, leaving a clear run for your sander, scraper, or plane.

Gang-sanding installed drawer fronts

If hand-planing turns you off (I have my days, believe me), try power-sanding the drawer fronts. But do it with all the drawers, even a solo drawer, in the case so you can level both drawers and case at the same time without worrying about excessively sanding individual components.

1. Slide the drawers into the case with the cabinet standing so they sit as fitted earlier. Without moving them, carefully wedge the drawers in place with slips of veneer. **A**

2. Lay the case on its back, and sand the entire face of the cabinet as you would a tabletop or other similarly large panel. You can use a belt sander to

WEDGED CLOSED. Slip a few strips of veneer into the gaps above and below the drawers to snug them into their openings, and break off any protruding strips.

SAND THE FACE AS ONE. An aggressive random-orbit sander makes quick work of leveling the drawers to the front of the case.

WEDGE REMOVER. Use a thin slip of steel to punch the shims through the gaps at the top of the drawer, freeing it from the case.

expedite the job, but it takes skill to maneuver the tool without creating dips, bumps, and scars. Some of today's modern random-orbit sanders have very aggressive sanding capabilities, and make quick work of this. **B**

3. If you did a good job of wedging, you won't easily remove the drawers once they're sanded flush.

Use a thin blank of steel or other hard material (a card scraper works great) to tap the wedges through the gaps at the tops of the drawer, pushing them into the case and freeing the drawers. **C** Finish up by removing any orbital marks on the faces by hand-sanding with the grain.

EASING EDGES

Easing the edges of your work is a simple task that can make a good project great. Sadly, it's often overlooked. Miss this step, and hard edges may splinter, causing hands to recoil as they pass over sharp edges. Not only do soft edges make your furniture more durable and inviting to touch, they highlight your good joints and flat surfaces by creating controlled shadow lines instead of the hard, mechanized, and often jagged angles and lines that tooling leaves. Be sure to ease all sharp edges, whether they're handled or simply seen.

You can cut larger bevels or roundovers using router bits or small planes. Alternatively, you can just hand-sand an edge until it has a subtle but consistent feel and look. For a fine line and more control, use a flat block of hard wood with fine sandpaper tightly wrapped around it. For example, use the block to kiss the corners of a drawer front, maintaining its crisp lines while softening the razor-like edge. Use the same block for reaching inside corners, which are notoriously difficult to sand by hand alone.

SHARP TO THE EYE, BUT NOT TO THE HAND. Keep your edges clean and crisp—but not sharp—by rounding them lightly with fine paper wrapped around a flat hardwood block.

MITER WITH PAPER. Use the edge of the block to reach into inside corners, creating a precise and handsome mitered intersection of the two chamfered edges.

Choosing Handles, Knobs, and Pulls

A comfortable, good-looking pull sets off a well-made drawer and can become the focal point of a case. Your style choices are endless, ranging from commercial handles and knobs to pulls you can make yourself. If you buy commercial versions, look for fine finishes and stout screws, bolts, and connecting hardware. When selecting iron, brass, copper, or bronze hardware, look for solid castings, as plated parts won't wear as well. Whatever you get, plan to spend some serious dough. Good hardware isn't cheap.

On the flip side, you can save money and create a one-of-a-kind look by making your own handles in a variety of designs, using the wood of your choice. Dense woods are typically best for this application, as are highly figured woods or woods with unusual color or markings. Now is the time to use some of that special stuff you've been stashing away in boxes and bins.

For the simplest of pulls, merely screw some wood strips to the face of your drawers from the backside. A turned, wooden knob with a lipped

BEAUTIFUL, STRONG AND EASY TO INSTALL. Commercial pulls, such as the solid-rod style handles shown here, are quick to install and easy on the hand.

STRIPS MAKE PULLS. Consecutive strips of wood on adjacent drawer fronts add a contemporary feel, and make effective pulls if you cut a slight bevel on the top and bottom edges for good grip.

HANDLE STYLES

Commercial Pulls

BRASS KNOB

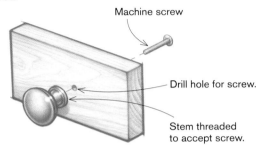

Machine screw

Drill hole for screw.

Stem threaded
to accept screw.

WIRE PULL

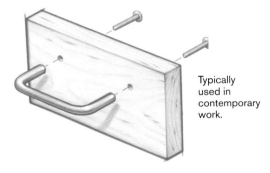

Typically
used in
contemporary
work.

DROP-BAIL PULL

Bail pivots downward
when at rest; typically
found in reproduction work.

Shop-Made Pulls

WOOD STRIP

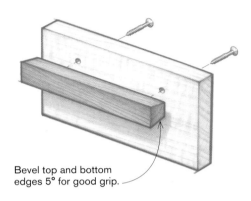

Bevel top and bottom
edges 5° for good grip.

TURNED, WEDGED KNOB

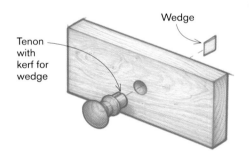

Wedge

Tenon
with
kerf for
wedge

CARVED PULL

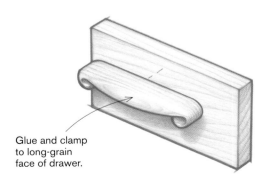

Glue and clamp
to long-grain
face of drawer.

AN INSTANT CLASSIC. This small, turned ebony knob will set off just about any drawer. Make it easy to grasp by tapering the body below the head so fingers can get a grip.

head or a tapered shank is a perennial favorite among furniture makers. It's comfortable to grasp and is easily turned on the lathe.

A carved pull makes a more personal statement, and can be shaped in any number of ways. Look at furniture in museums and books for inspiration for your pulls, or sketch out something new.

Attaching Metal Pulls

Pulls with metal posts, including wire pulls and drop-bail pulls, are almost as common to drawers as soap is to the shower. But you don't have to settle for blasé versions. You can find unique and quite extraordinary metal pulls if you shop around. What all these types of pulls have in common is the method by which they attach to the drawer, typically with bolts that pass through holes drilled in the drawer front and into the pulls'

CHARMED BY CARVING. The hand-tooled surface on this pull, carved with chisels and gouges, adds a personal touch. A clamped glue joint is sufficient to attach the pull to the drawer as long as you orient the grain of both in the same direction.

PERFECT HARDWARE HOLES. A simple plywood jig helps locate and align the holes for the pulls. Align the jig with marks on the cabinet, then hold or clamp it while you drill through it into the drawer front.

A

posts. Installation is very simple, with the only trick being drilling the bolt holes accurately so the machine screws that hold them are evenly spaced and the pull is properly aligned to the drawer front. Happily, an easy-to-make jig ensures success.

1. Make the jig by laying out the spacing of the pull's bolt holes onto a piece of ¾-in.-thick plywood sized to the width of your drawer, using a square to extend the holes' centerlines onto the ends of the jig. To ensure the holes are perpendicular, bore them on the drill press.

2. To use the jig, mark the desired height of the holes on the case side or partition, and then place the jig over the drawer front so the centerlines align and drill through the jig and the drawer front. **A** If all your drawers are the same width, you can use the same jig to drill all the holes. Make a separate jig for drawers of different widths.

Turned and Wedged Knob

Turning pulls on the lathe is a mainstay of furniture work, and many woodworkers keep a lathe in the shop just for this purpose, even if they don't do a lot of other turning. One of the strongest methods for securing a turned pull to a drawer front is to turn a tenon on one end, fit it into a hole drilled through the drawer front, and then wedge the tenon from behind, locking it into the drawer front.

1. Start with a blank that's oversized in length, and turn a series of pulls between centers, roughing out their overall shape. At this point, size each tenon as closely as possible to the diameter of the drill bit you'll be using. **A** I typically turn ½-in.-dia. tenons for medium-size knobs, and ⅜ in. tenons for smaller pulls.

2. Part off each knob and finish shaping and smoothing the head after temporarily mounting the tenon snugly in a hole drilled in a wooden faceplate mounted on the headstock. **B**

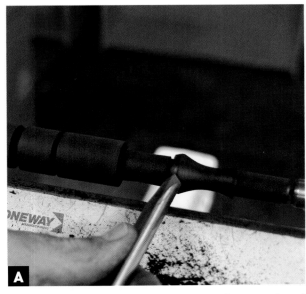

TURN THE TENONS. Use a narrow gouge to shape a series of pulls on a blank mounted between centers. Turn the tenon about ¼ in. longer than the thickness of the drawer front, and size it to the diameter of the drill bit you'll be using.

SHAPE THE FACE. Mount the tenon into a hole drilled in a wooden faceplate, and finish the top of the head with the same gouge.

C

HOLE STOPS SPLITTING. Holding the pull in a V-block on the drill press, use a ⅛-in.-dia. bit to drill a small hole through the center of the tenon near the head.

3. To prevent splitting the tenon when you drive home the wedge, drill a ⅛-in.-dia. hole through the tenon near the head of the pull, using a V-block to support the work. **C**

4. Keeping the knob in the V-block, insert a ⅛-in.-dia. bamboo skewer (available at grocery stores) into the hole to serve as a gauge to help you align the hole parallel to the blade of your bandsaw. Holding the knob firmly, push it into the blade to saw a kerf for the wedge, stopping when you reach the hole. **D & E**

5. Saw a slim wedge to fit the kerf, using a resilient wood such as oak for strength.

6. Use the drill press to bore the hole in the drawer front, making sure to back up the underside with a scrap block for a clean exit hole. **F**

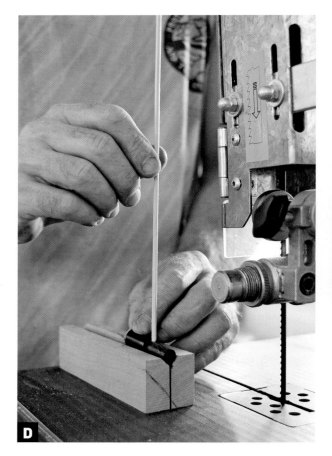

D

E

ALIGN AND SAW. Align the hole parallel to the blade using a long dowel, then hold the knob firmly and saw a kerf along the center of the tenon, stopping at the hole.

7. It's wise to test-fit each knob before gluing it into its respective front. You may need to sand the tenon lightly with a strip of flexible, cloth-backed sandpaper or with a safe-edged file. Spread some glue in the hole and on the tenon, and push the tenon into the hole so that the kerf is at right angles to the grain of the drawer front. This prevents the wedge from splitting the drawer. Put a dab of glue on the wedge, and start tapping it into the kerf. **G** Overly aggressive tapping can split the tenon, as well as the knob. So take light taps, and listen: When you hear a dull sound, the wedge is seated. Stop tapping.

8. Once the glue has dried, saw off the protruding tenon and wedge, and sand the surface smooth. **H** Although the joint is rarely seen, it's quite attractive and ensures your knobs stay in place for years to come.

F

DRILL FOR THE TENON. Clamp a scrap block under the drawer front, then drill the hole using a bit equal to the tenon's diameter.

G

TAP AND LISTEN. Align the knob's kerf at right angles to the grain of the drawer, and carefully tap in the wedge. Listen for a change in sound—usually a duller note—to detect when the wedge is seated.

H

WEDGE WORK. The wedge spreads the tenon into the walls of the hole, making a very tight joint. The decorative contrast is nice, too.

Drawer Stops

The last step before applying a finish to your drawers is to consider how and where to stop inward drawer travel within the case. You may also want to install outward stops to prevent accidentally yanking a drawer free and spilling its contents. In addition, you may need to secure a drawer's contents by adding a locking mechanism. There are several ready-made pieces of hardware that will help you, and plenty of shop-savvy tricks for making your own devices.

Drawer closing stops

Most commercial metal slides include springs, detents, or sloped areas that will automatically close your drawer and keep it shut. But a wood-to-wood drawer requires a little planning on your part to make sure it stops in the case where you want it to.

On an overlay or lipped drawer, the back of the drawer front will stop the drawer when it contacts the front of the case. The easiest method for stopping inset drawers is to dimension the case and drawer parts so the back of the drawer contacts the back of the case when it's pushed in. To position a

STOPPING A DRAWER

Overlay or Lipped Front

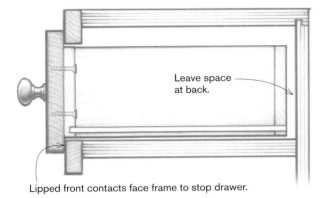

Leave space at back.

Lipped front contacts face frame to stop drawer.

Extended Bottom

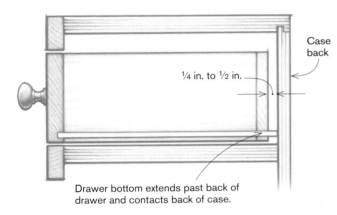

Case back

1/4 in. to 1/2 in.

Drawer bottom extends past back of drawer and contacts back of case.

Wood Strip

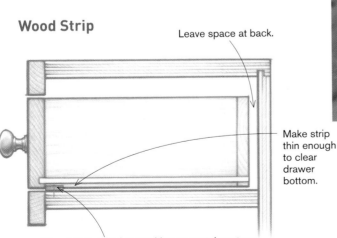

Leave space at back.

Make strip thin enough to clear drawer bottom.

Wood strip nailed to partition or stretcher stops drawer by contacting back of drawer front.

drawer front more precisely at the front of the case, one option is to extend the drawer bottom so it contacts the case back. This allows you to fine-tune the fit by shaving only the rear edge of the bottom until the front of the drawer sits exactly where you want it.

A traditional method for stopping drawers is to glue and nail small wood stop-blocks to the rail directly behind the drawer front. To locate the blocks accurately, you can set a marking gauge to the thickness of the drawer front, then use it to scribe a line on the case. However, the downside of this and all other wood-to-wood contact can be an annoying *smack* every time you close the drawer. You can soften the blow using a variety of bumpers, including commercially available self-adhesive felt

STOPPED BY WOOD. Furniture maker Kelly Mehler nails one or two strips of wood to the front rail on his side table to stop the back of the drawer front. Orient the end grain facing out for strength.

LEATHER IS BETTER.
Drawer stops faced with leather impart a softer, quieter feel than wood alone. Glue the leather to the stops, and then glue the stops to the stretcher.

BUMP IT CLOSED. Bumpers come in a range of materials, including felt, cork, rubber, and soft plastic. Attached to the rear of the drawer box or drawer front, they'll cushion the blow of a drawer closing.

or rubber pads. Attach them to the back of the drawer front on overlay or lipped drawers, or fix them to the back of a drawer that contacts the rear of the case. For a shop-made fix, use yellow or white glue to adhere leather to a wood stop strip, then glue and clamp the strip to the drawer stretcher.

Drawer opening stops

While it's convenient to be able to remove a drawer from the case for occasional cleaning or periodic lubrication, it's smart to provide some form of stop that prevents accidentally pulling the drawer all the way out and spilling its contents. Commercial metal slides incorporate stops, but wood-to-wood drawers require some kind of shop-made mechanism.

If your case includes a frame above the drawer, there are a couple of approaches you can take. The first is to screw a simple, pivoting wooden block to the back of the drawer. Oriented vertically, it catches on the rear of the face frame when the drawer is extended, but it can easily be pivoted horizontally to remove the drawer. If you like, you can take the opposite approach and attach a pivoting block to the rear of an overhead rail instead.

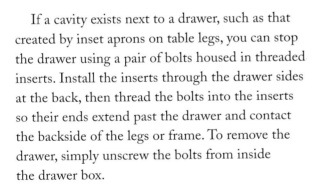

OUTWARD STOP BLOCKS. To prevent accidentally yanking a drawer all the way out, you can screw to the drawer back a pivoting stop that will engage an overhead rail when the drawer is extended. Alternatively, you can screw a similar stop to the overhead rail to engage the drawer back.

If a cavity exists next to a drawer, such as that created by inset aprons on table legs, you can stop the drawer using a pair of bolts housed in threaded inserts. Install the inserts through the drawer sides at the back, then thread the bolts into the inserts so their ends extend past the drawer and contact the backside of the legs or frame. To remove the drawer, simply unscrew the bolts from inside the drawer box.

OUTWARD STOP BOLTS. A pair of machine screws extending through threaded inserts in the drawer sides will stop against the inner face of an overhanging face frame or offset table legs. Simply retract the bolts to remove the drawer.

Drawer Locks

If security is a concern, locking a drawer is something to consider. There are two primary types of locks: the cylinder lock and the half-mortise lock. The cylinder lock is much easier to install and is typically used for contemporary work. The half-mortise lock is found on many antique or reproduction pieces, and requires careful layout and mortising for successful installation.

Installing a cylinder lock

1. Mark out for the cylinder location, which is typically centered across the width of a drawer.

2. Drill a hole through the drawer front to accept the cylinder. Most types can be surface-mounted to the back of the drawer front, so you don't have to bother cutting a mortise into the back side.

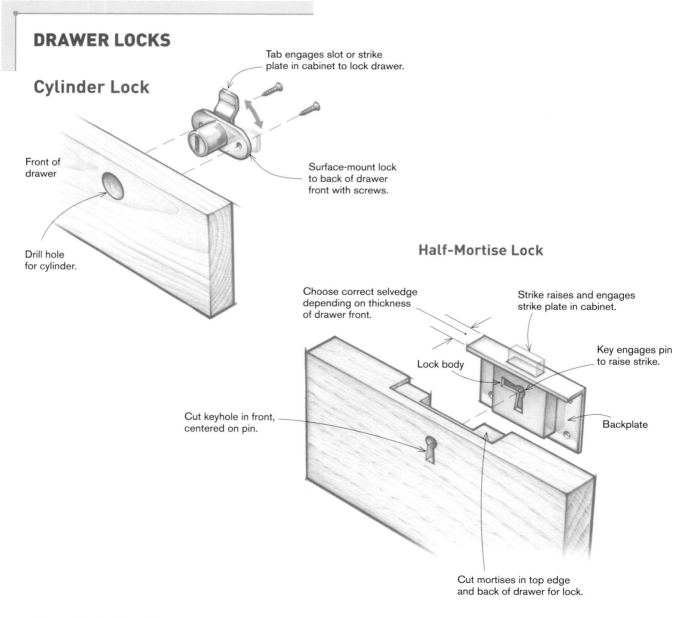

DRAWER LOCKS

Cylinder Lock

Tab engages slot or strike plate in cabinet to lock drawer.

Front of drawer

Surface-mount lock to back of drawer front with screws.

Drill hole for cylinder.

Half-Mortise Lock

Choose correct selvedge depending on thickness of drawer front.

Strike raises and engages strike plate in cabinet.

Lock body

Key engages pin to raise strike.

Cut keyhole in front, centered on pin.

Backplate

Cut mortises in top edge and back of drawer for lock.

3. After screwing the lock in place, transfer the strike location to the case and cut a mortise to accept the strike. For better security, install a strike plate over the mortise.

Installing a half-mortise lock

Select a half-mortise lock whose selvage suits the thickness of the drawer you'll be using. Plan to leave about ⅛ in. of space between the edge of the selvage and the drawer face. You can drill and saw the keyhole through the drawer front and leave it as is, or install a surface-mounted or inset escutcheon. A bare keyhole has a clean and more subdued look, but the hole must be cut crisply to look good. Escutcheons, which are more traditional, protect the drawer front from key scratches while dressing up the face and hiding any keyhole irregularities.

1. Lay out the lock pin location with the tip of an awl, measuring the distance between the selvage and the center of the pin.

2. If you're using a surface-mounted escutcheon, you can drill through the front with a bit that matches the diameter of the keyhole, then tack the escutcheon to the front of the drawer after installing the lock.

Alternatively, if you're using an inset escutcheon, first bore a hole that matches the outer diameter of the rounded part of the escutcheon, drilling to a depth that's slightly less than the thickness of the escutcheon. Holding the escutcheon in position, trace around its skirted end with a sharp knife, and chisel this area to the same depth as the hole. At this point, you can glue the escutcheon in place with a dab of cyanoacrylate glue, tapping it in place. After the adhesive has cured, sand the surface flush. Then drill through your original awl mark for the key with a brad-point bit and cut out the skirt with a coping saw. **A**

3. Use a ruler and square to lay out the mortise for the lock body, being careful to align it with the keyhole. Rout or chisel the mortise, making it

OPEN THE KEYHOLE. After cutting the recess for the inset escutcheon and gluing it in place, drill through the rounded head area as shown here, then use a coping saw to cut out the interior of the skirted area.

CHISEL TO FIT. Cut three mortises to fit the lock: one for the lock body, one for the backplate, and a third for the selvage along the top edge of the drawer.

NEAT AND SIMPLE. A brass escutcheon is the only visible part of the lock from the front, with the lock plate flush to the top edge of the drawer.

a tad deeper than the combined thickness of the body and backplate and a bit wider than the body's width. It's okay if the mortise is a bit crude; the backplate will cover any gaps. Just be sure to leave sufficient material for the mounting screws.

4. Lay out the mortise for the backplate. Place the body in its mortise, centering the keyhole, and trace around the backplate with a knife. Rout the majority of this shallow mortise to a depth that matches the thickness of the plate, then carefully pare your knife lines with a chisel. **B**

5. Lay out the selvage mortise on the top edge of the drawer by pressing the lock in the previously cut mortises and tracing around the selvage with a sharp knife. Rout and chisel the mortise as before. If necessary, chisel the backplate mortise a little wider so the selvage seats fully into its mortise, then screw the lock to the drawer. The finished lock should be even with the top of the drawer. **C**

6. Install the drawer, mark where the strike hits the cabinet, and cut the strike mortise. A striker plate adds security and class.

Lubricating Drawers

To keep a sweet-running drawer running smoothly, it should be lubricated so parts glide easily. Metal slides will benefit from occasional cleaning and re-greasing of the bearings to keep the parts in good working order. Wood-to-wood drawers need a little more attention. On existing wood drawers, an annual coat of paste wax rubbed on all the bearing surfaces and then buffed off will improve the action significantly.

For a new drawer, the same holds true, except you need to provide a suitable base surface for the wax because bare wood doesn't fit the bill. The best approach is to give all the bearing surfaces a light coat of finish before waxing. But be careful here: You don't want to build up a heavy film finish of lacquer or urethane, as it will eventually wear through, creating clumps and clogs that will cause the drawer to stick. I recommend a light coat of shellac on all wear surfaces, including the parts of the case that the drawer will contact. **A & B** Once the finish has dried, use a fine nylon-abrasive pad coated with paste wax to smooth the surface, and then buff away all excess wax with a soft cloth. Now you've got a drawer that really moves.

SHELLAC AS A BASE. To provide a good surface for subsequent waxing, give all the bearing surfaces of your drawers a light coat of shellac, including drawer sides and case runners.

4 SPECIAL DRAWERS AND DETAILS

- *Special Drawers*
- *Pullouts*
- *Trays*
- *Dividing Drawer Interiors*
- *Lining a Drawer*
- *French-Fitting a Drawer*

Th**his chapter is designed to take you beyond the basics,** so you can build drawers that depart from the norm. It includes drawers with eye-catching details, drawers that perform unusual functions, and drawers whose interiors are divided for specific storage solutions. I'll also discuss "secret" drawers that hide themselves from prying eyes, and even drawers that simply look cool.

You can build some or all of the designs you find here, or simply dream and cogitate on them if you wish. Either way, use these ideas as a springboard for your imagination, so you can construct extraordinary drawers and instill in your projects a higher plane of woodworking, with finer furniture as the result. Above all, have fun!

Special Drawers

Sometimes the simplest approach produces the best result, such as adding a bit of detail to make otherwise plain drawers something special. For example, Sam Maloof's cabinet displays a series of slightly inset drawers fitted inside the case dividers, which themselves have been rounded over along their edges. It took very little extra work and, in fact, it makes fitting the drawers much easier because they don't have to be flush with the case. The rounded edges and inset drawers create a look that's anything but standard fare. The chest shows how small details can dramatically change the look of a piece.

On the other hand, constructing special drawers for specific storage needs, creating curves and fanciful shapes, making extra-small drawers, or incorporating hidden drawers can add fun and function to any type of cabinet. Your only cost is time and effort.

MALOOF ROUNDOVER. Slightly inset drawers in Sam Maloof's walnut cabinet are flanked by case partitions with rounded edges, creating strong shadow lines and a much easier fit for the drawers.

File drawers

Big drawers are usually a pain, because they're generally difficult to keep organized and stuff gets lost in the back. Not so for file drawers. Here, big is good because tracks or rods mounted at the top of the drawer hold hanging file folders, keeping all your paperwork well organized and accessible at a moment's notice.

There's not much to building file drawers, and very little special hardware is needed. Be sure to use heavy-duty full-extension metal slides to handle the extra weight and provide access to the back of the drawer. To accommodate hanging file folders, you can buy plastic folder hangers sized to slip over the top edges of ½-in.-thick sides. Alternatively, you can use flat bar stock or ¼-in.-dia. brass or steel rod.

When building a file drawer, keep a few important dimensions in mind: The drawer must be at least 9½ in. tall inside to clear the hanging files, and the box itself should be sized to the type of hanging folders you plan to use, whether standard letter-size or legal-size folders. Dimension the drawer so the centerline between hanging bars is either 12¼ in. (for letter-size folders) or 15¼ in. (for legal files). If you like, you could equip the drawer with both filing options.

FILE DRAWER LAYOUT

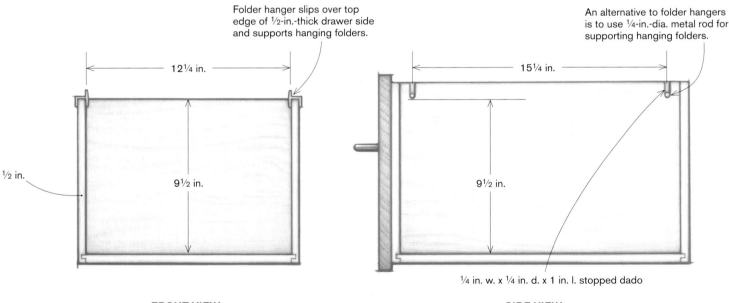

Drawer Box for Letter-Size Files

Folder hanger slips over top edge of ½-in.-thick drawer side and supports hanging folders.

12¼ in.

½ in.

9½ in.

FRONT VIEW

Drawer Box for Legal-Size Files

An alternative to folder hangers is to use ¼-in.-dia. metal rod for supporting hanging folders.

15¼ in.

9½ in.

¼ in. w. x ¼ in. d. x 1 in. l. stopped dado

SIDE VIEW

TWO FILES IN ONE. This lateral file drawer sports brass rods housed in stopped dadoes that can be repositioned to hang either letter- or legal-size file folders.

CURVED IN BACK, TOO. The curved drawer front in this chest of drawers is made from a series of wood laminates pressed together over a bending form, then faced in curly maple veneer.

Curved-front drawers

Bow-front chests, bombé chests, serpentine chests, and many other types of furniture feature curved drawer fronts that add tremendous flair to a piece. The simplest method for producing a curved-front drawer is to work with a solid blank, sawing the curve on only the outside face using the bandsaw, and leaving the inside face flat and straight.

For a classier look, you can curve the inside face of the drawer to match the outside, creating a curved drawer front of uniform thickness. You can make this type of curve from a series of wood laminates, gluing them together over a bending form and pressing them in a shop-made veneer press or in a vacuum bag. This approach lets you use prized wood veneers on the show face for maximum effect. Joinery is straightforward, and can incorporate rabbets or dovetails at the corners, though you'll need to support the workpiece with scrap blocks to steady it if you saw the joints on the tablesaw.

For a double curve, such as for a serpentine drawer front, you can again make a bending form to the desired shape, and then press the laminates onto the form. Make the front oversized in width

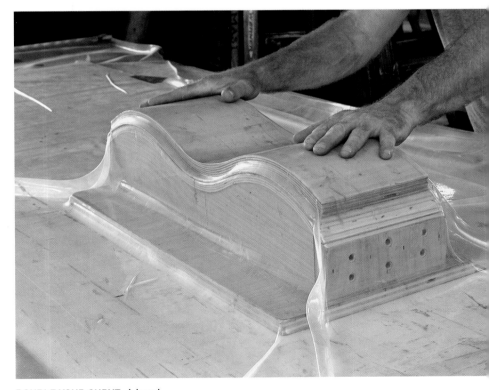

DOUBLE YOUR CURVE. A bending form with a double curve lets you create a serpentine front by pressing laminates in a vacuum bag.

TRIM IT SQUARE. After veneering the face and back and ripping the oversized blank to width, crosscut it to length using a sled on the tablesaw.

BANDSAW THE TAILS. Two of the three tails in each drawer side are curved to match the cove of the drawer front, and are easily cut on the bandsaw.

and length, apply veneer to the front and the back (to balance out the veneers and prevent warp), then trim it to final size on the tablesaw.

Cove-front drawers

For a real "gee-whiz" effect, you can add another type of curve to a drawer front in the form of a cove cut into its face, then join the sides with half-blind dovetails that curve to reflect the coved front for a unique, decorative touch.

1. Mill the cove in the front either with a large router or shaper bit, or by angling the work across the tablesaw blade with a makeshift fence clamped to the desired angle.

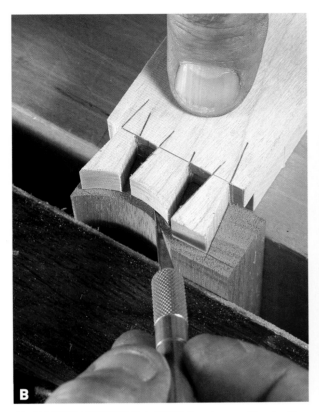

GOUGE CUTS THE CURVE. Chisel out the waste around the pins with narrow chisels, using a gouge of the appropriate sweep to create the curved areas at the front.

FOLLOW THE CURVE WITH A KNIFE. As when making traditional half-blind dovetails, use the sawn tail piece to lay out and scribe the pins in the coved front.

2. Lay out the tails on the drawer sides to accommodate the cove on the front, and use the bandsaw to cut to your profile. **A** If necessary, you can clean up and refine the curve on the end by touching it up on a spindle sander after sawing.

3. Scribe the pins from the tails, just as you would traditional half-blind dovetails (see Chapter 2), including the curved area at the front. **B** As with traditional dovetails, use a handsaw to saw as much of the pins as possible, then clean out the waste with chisels. The only tricky part is where the tail sockets curve at the front. Choose a gouge of the correct sweep (or curvature) for this cut, and tap down into the wood to define these areas. **C**

4. Glue up and fit the drawer, and listen to friends say, "How'd you do that?" **D**

COVED DOVETAILS. The ends of the tails on the sides of this narrow drawer follow the coved area on the drawer front, adding a special effect unlike any other.

TAPERED DRAWERS

Furniture maker Gary van Rawlins decided to try his hand at building tapered drawer sides after some curious Shaker drawers he'd seen in an old book inspired him. The effect is more aesthetic than functional, producing a pleasing slope on the insides of the drawer and a thinner, more delicate top edge. However, in true Shaker fashion, there's a practical side, too: The bottom of the sides are thicker, providing more wear surface for tracking the drawer.

Joinery is straightforward if done in the right sequence. First, lay out and cut the dovetails in the sides, then taper them by passing them through the thickness planer on a sloped ramp. The precise angle isn't critical; a slope of about 3 degrees creates a pleasing proportion. After tapering the sides, use them to lay out and cut the joints in the front and back, scribing around the wedge-shaped sides to lay out the pins and the angled baselines. Once you glue up the drawer, the outsides are square, so no special fitting is required to mount the drawer into the case.

INSIDE SLOPE. Drawer sides that taper from about 1/2 in. at the bottom to 3/16 in. at the top edges provide a delicate feel to these small drawers, while providing more bearing surface on the bottom edges.

Teeny tiny drawers

Sometimes a really small drawer is in order, whether it's for a keepsake box, jewelry box, or even a scale model of a piece of furniture you might wish to make. The challenge when making such items is cutting joints that look good and fit well, since everything is magnified when working on such a small scale, making precision count. Nothing could be truer than when cutting diminutive dovetails.

Furniture maker Yeung Chan's small wooden chest is a prime example of how you can work small yet accurately. To cut the half-blind and through dovetail joints in his drawers, Yeung uses special narrow chisels he designed (available from Lee Valley Tools) as well as a special 32 teeth-per-inch Japanese dozuki saw with a blade that's only 0.008 in. thin (available from The Japan Woodworker).

With these two specialized tools, you can cut joints so small that you may need a magnifying glass to appreciate them.

Secret drawers

For fun, and because everybody loves a secret, you can try your hand at making hidden drawers. The trick is to look for "extra" space in a cabinet, and then outfit that space for a secret compartment or a set of special drawers. Many cabinets have the necessary space at the bottom, where you can incorporate a wider bottom rail that conceals a "false" bottom raised above the actual case bottom.

Using the same idea of space at the bottom of a case, you can include small hidden drawers to give your "secret" even more punch. I credit my woodworking mentor, cabinetmaker Frank Klausz, for

DIMINUTIVE DOVETAILS. Standing less than 5 in. tall, this solid-wood chest made by furniture maker Yeung Chan features tiny dovetailed drawers created by using a 1/16-in. chisel and a very fine-cutting Japanese backsaw.

LOOK DOWN LOW. The compartments behind the drawers at the bottom of this walnut chest are hidden from view by a wide, lower rail and by ¼-in.-thick "false" plywood bottoms raised above the real case bottom.

SECRET DRAWER ANATOMY

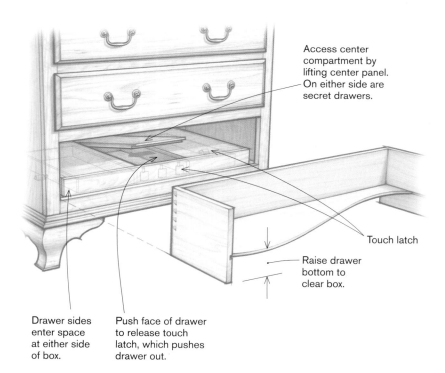

Access center compartment by lifting center panel. On either side are secret drawers.

Touch latch

Raise drawer bottom to clear box.

Drawer sides enter space at either side of box.

Push face of drawer to release touch latch, which pushes drawer out.

describing the following arrangement I used when designing a traditional linen press cabinet years ago.

The lowest drawer has a raised bottom, which provides room for a compartment, or large box, mounted to the bottom of the case. There are three panels across the top of the box. Accessing the drawers is a trick. There's a removable center panel flanked by two fixed panels. To remove the center panel, you press down on its front to activate three touch-latches (see "Touch-latch trays," p. 84) and then remove the panel to access a center compartment.

If a thief ever gets this far, he'll most likely think he's solved the mystery and move on, especially if the wise owner places something semi-valuable in this center compartment. However, the side walls of the cavity are actually the fronts of two small drawers, which you open by pressing them inward to release more touch-latches. Pull out the drawers and remove them through the center opening and, voila! Inside each drawer are the real collectibles—including a spare key to the cabinet should the owner ever lose the original.

Pullouts

You can have more than just drawers going in and out of your furniture and cabinets if you leave space for some equally useful sliding gear, such as pullouts and trays. Pullouts, sometimes called rollouts, are nothing more than drawers that reside behind doors, quietly out of view until you open the cabinet. They're easy to build, and add versatility to the storage and function of a case or piece of furniture.

Pullouts are typically hung on metal slides, and provide much more convenient access to a case's contents than do standard cabinet shelves. An entire cabinet full of pullouts can be especially handy in a kitchen, but pullouts make just as much sense in fine furniture or in other stand-alone pieces. They work with metal slides or as wood-to-wood drawers, and usually don't need any fancy pull hardware to access.

Scooped pullouts

It's common to build average-size pullouts in a cabinet because, just like ordinary drawers, items can get lost in a big, cavernous box. However, you can have your cake (a big drawer) and eat it, too (store lots of items—and actually get to 'em), if you build a large drawer with a narrow front and scooped sides that rise to meet a tall back. With this arrangement, the entire contents of the drawer are easy to see, especially if you place taller items at the back, and bulky items won't fall or tip out because the high sides and back contain them.

To build a series of scooped drawers, you can employ a template-routing technique that speeds up the process.

1. Make left and right templates to the precise shape of the scooped sides from plywood, bandsawing and then fairing their double-curved shapes with rasps, files, and sandpaper. Since the curves are identical on both sides, differing only in that the joints are cut into opposing faces, you'll save time if you fair only one template, then use it to template-rout its mate. Once you're happy with the contours, nail registration fences to the edges of the templates.

2. Cut the joints in the drawer parts, including the side blanks, and then position each side in its respective template and trace the template's contours onto the side. **A**

GET IT QUICK. The author's pantry of pullout drawers behind sliding doors makes it a snap to get to the case's contents.

TALL, YET MANAGEABLE. A deep and tall pullout is easy to organize and access if you keep the front narrow while scooping the sides and incorporating a tall back.

3. Bandsaw each side so it's slightly proud of the traced line.

4. Remount the side in the template and use a pattern bit (a straight bit fitted with a ball bearing of equal diameter) in the router table to rout the side to the exact shape of the template. **B** Repeat the template-routing process for as many pullout drawers as your storage needs require.

TRACE IT FIRST. After cutting the drawer joints, trace the outline of each routing template onto a drawer side.

NOW ROUT TO THE LINE. The bearing on the bit follows the contours of the template to create a drawer side the exact same size.

Trays

There are arguably just as many types of trays as there are drawers, and all add myriad functions to what otherwise might be rather plain cabinets, tables, or desktops. In its basic form, a tray is a flat panel, typically made from ¼-in.-, ½-in.-, or ¾-in.-thick plywood edged with solid wood. It slides out of the case to provide temporary support for items or to serve as an impromptu surface for writing or other intermittent chores, and then tucks back into its opening afterward. You can install it in the case as you would a drawer, using metal slides or employing any of the drawer-sliding techniques you would use for normal drawers. For specialized trays, read on.

Touch-latch trays

This small, leathered-covered tray is similar to a standard tray, except that it springs open when you push on it, thanks to a spring-loaded touch-latch mechanism at its rear. To keep the tray closed, a magnet on the end of the spring-loaded cylinder contacts a metal plate screwed to the rear of the tray.

HOW A TOUCH LATCH WORKS

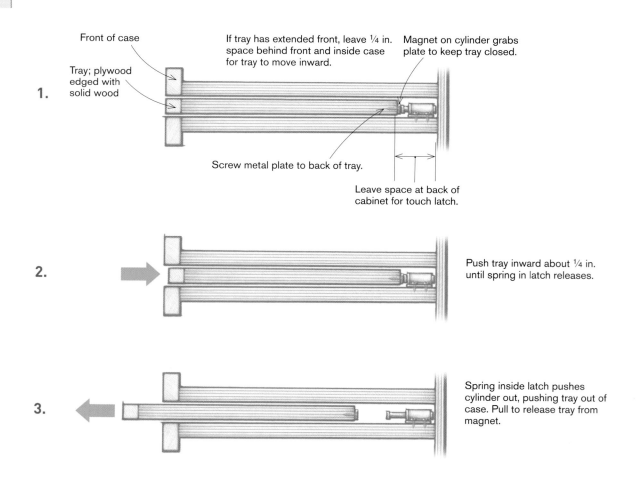

1.

Front of case

Tray; plywood edged with solid wood

If tray has extended front, leave ¼ in. space behind front and inside case for tray to move inward.

Magnet on cylinder grabs plate to keep tray closed.

Screw metal plate to back of tray.

Leave space at back of cabinet for touch latch.

2.

Push tray inward about ¼ in. until spring in latch releases.

3.

Spring inside latch pushes cylinder out, pushing tray out of case. Pull to release tray from magnet.

Fitting any tray, lid, or door with a touch latch is straightforward if you keep a few things in mind. Make the tray short enough to allow space behind it for the mechanism. Also, if the front of a tray or drawer overlaps its sides (or if a lid or door is backed by a divider), allow enough room behind for the "throw" of the spring-loaded catch. Just make sure the piece can move inward about ¼ in. when pushed. If necessary, inset dividers or other interior case parts.

Make and fit the tray to the case, using a wood-to-wood slide mechanism, which can be as simple as the tray sliding in grooves cut in the case. (Don't use metal slides; their closure mechanism prevents the touch latch from working properly.) After installing the tray and the metal plate, screw the latch to the cabinet case so that the magnet is contacting the metal plate with the cylinder retracted. To open the tray, simply push it in about ¼ in. This releases the cylinder, which pushes the tray forward from the case about ½ in.—just enough to allow you to grasp the leading edge to pull it the rest of the way out.

In fact, with a lightweight tray like this, a quick, deft poke will cause it to spring almost all the way out by itself, which is very cool. In general, touch-latches work best for more lightweight components with narrow edges, like relatively thin trays and doors. They aren't a good choice for heavier components, such as standard drawers, but they work well for small drawers with fronts no thicker than ¼ in.

METAL TO MAGNET. To keep the tray closed, a magnet on the end of the touch-latch cylinder contacts a metal plate screwed to the back of the tray.

TOUCH-LATCH ACTION. Pushing the tray about ¼ in. inward releases the spring-loaded touch-latch cylinder at the rear of the tray. This drives the tray out of the case about ½ in., allowing you to pull it out the rest of the way.

Keyboard trays

This digital age demands a lot of time spent at computers, so a comfortable spot for a keyboard is high on many people's list. What better way to get comfy in front of your computer than to make your own custom keyboard tray from glorious wood instead of homogenized, soulless plastic?

First, buy the slide hardware, which is readily available from many woodworking catalogs. The best hardware comes with a tray-holding mechanism that pulls out, swivels, tilts, and raises and lowers, letting you optimize the position of your keyboard.

1. Make the tray from solid ¾-in.-thick wood or veneered plywood edged with solid wood, dimensioning it to hold your keyboard and leaving space for a mouse or other input device.

WOOD IS GOOD. Shape a wrist rest for comfort, rounding over its edges with router bits or with a plane, and screw it to the tray from underneath.

GUIDED BY A PLATE. Mount the plate that guides the tray-holding mechanism by screwing it under the work surface, positioning it as far forward as possible to provide maximum reach for your keyboard.

SLIDE DEVICE HOLDS TRAY. Slide the mechanism onto the plate, and then mount the tray on top of it by driving screws from underneath.

MAKE IT YOUR OWN. Once installed, a good keyboard mechanism allows you to pull out or push in the tray, swivel it, adjust its angle, and raise or lower its height to suit your individual typing or mousing style.

2. Shape a wrist rest from wood. Round over its edges for comfort, and screw it to the front edge of the tray. **A** Complete the tray by applying a durable finish such as lacquer or urethane.

3. Mount the plate that guides the hardware to the underside of your desk or workspace, aligning its leading edge with the front edge of the desk to maximize the tray's reach. **B** Insert the sliding mechanism onto the plate and mount the tray to the mechanism by driving screws from underneath. **C** Once installed, fine-tune the tray and its support mechanism by adjusting its height and angle. **D**

TV swivels

For TV addicts who want the best-possible view, or anyone who wants a good look regardless of the seating arrangement in a room, it's smart to install a platform that allows you to swivel your tube for a picture-perfect angle. If you buy a swivel that comes with metal slide hardware, you can also get at the back of the set more easily to fuss with wiring and other connections.

As always, buy the hardware first, then build the tray to fit over the swivel.

1. Make the tray from ¾-in.-thick veneered plywood, sizing it to accommodate your set and the cabinet or fixed shelf where it will reside. Miter the back corners of the tray so it won't bind in the cabinet when the swivel is rotated, and then glue a wood strip to the front, making it wide enough to conceal the hardware, minus about ¼ in. for clearance. **A** Apply the finish of your choice.

2. Screw the swivel's metal platform to the underside of the tray. **B**

3. Install the assembly to the shelf by bolting the slides in place. **C** Now get ready for some swiveling action!

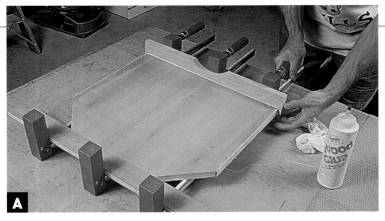

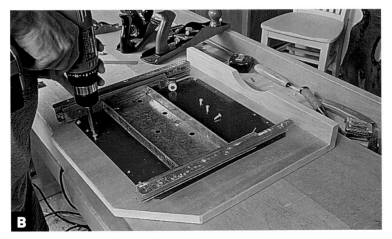

EDGE IT WITH WOOD. Glue a wide strip of solid wood to the front of the tray, with a cutout for a pull. A wide caul at the back gives the clamps purchase.

ATTACH THE HARDWARE. Screw the swivel mechanism to the underside of the tray, making sure the tray is centered and the slides don't contact the wood edge at front when the hardware swivels.

BOLTS ARE BETTER. Use bolts, not screws, to connect the slide hardware to a fixed shelf to support the weight of the TV.

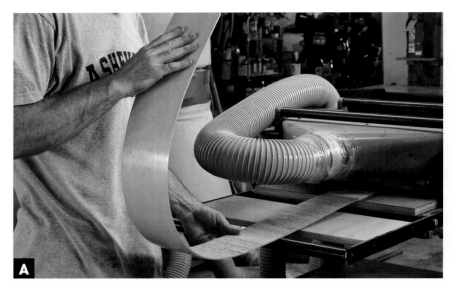

BEND IT YOURSELF. Make plywood bend easily by planing away one of the face veneers. Install a smooth panel on the bed of the planer to prevent gouging or rough cuts.

HELPING HANDS. Get a pal to help you glue the plywood to the edge of the tray. Staple all along the tray's edge and at its abutted ends, which should be centered over a bracket.

NO NAILS, JUST LOTS OF CLAMPS. Clamp a second layer of plywood to the first layer, using an additional piece wrapped around the second layer to help distribute clamp pressure.

Turntables

A turntable, also called a Lazy Susan, is a great addition inside a cabinet where you want to store a lot of small or medium-size items such as spice jars or drinking mugs. Buy the turntable hardware first, and then bandsaw or rout a circle for the tray from ½-in.-thick hardwood plywood, sizing it to the case where it will live. I like to add a wood lipping to the outside of the tray so items don't fall or slide off, and I start by making my own bendable edging from standard ¼-in. plywood.

1. Install a smooth plywood platform on the bed of your thickness planer to cover the bed rollers, then plane off one of the outer veneer layers from the plywood to expose the grain of the interior ply, which must run perpendicular to the edge of the tray. **A** With one outer ply gone, your plywood will bend to a diameter as tight as 10 in. or even less.

2. Glue and nail four plywood brackets to the top of the plywood circle in an equidistant pattern, and flush with the edges of the tray. Now glue and staple a preliminary layer of bending plywood to the

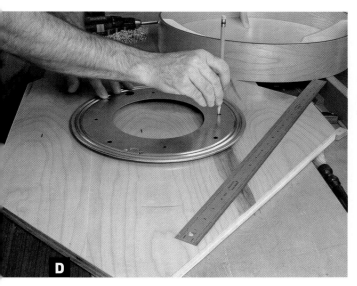

D SCREW IT AND MARK THROUGH IT. After centering and screwing the turntable to the shelf, mark through the hardware to locate an access hole for screwing the tray to the turntable.

E SCREW FROM BELOW. Attach the tray to the shelf by driving screws through the access hole, working upside down and spinning the shelf to locate each hole.

edge of the tray and to the brackets, with its "good" side facing in. **B**

3. Glue a second layer of bending plywood to the first, this time using as many clamps as you can muster instead of staples, and orienting the face veneer to the outside. **C** Once the glue has dried, the lamination has great strength, and provides a resilient and long-lasting edging.

4. Carefully center the turntable on the shelf, screw it fast, then mark for an access hole for the screws that will attach the turntable to the tray. **D** Remove the turntable and drill a ¾ in. hole through the shelf at your mark.

5. Remount the turntable to the shelf and, with the shelf upside down and the tray centered below it, drive screws through the turntable hardware and into the tray using the access hole. To find each hole in the hardware, simply rotate the shelf around the tray. **E** Once all the screws are in, you're ready to install the turntable assembly into the cabinet. **F**

F TAKE 'ER FOR A SPIN. With the hardware fixed to the shelf, your turntable is ready to spin and the assembly can be installed into the case.

DIVIDED BY ITSELF. The interior depth and width of the drawers in this media center are carefully sized to hold specific items, such as back-to-back rows of video tapes.

Dividing Drawer Interiors

A drawer's utility can increase by leaps and bounds if you build it with its intended contents in mind. In some instances, you can make the most of a special-purpose drawer simply by building it to a size that perfectly accommodates specific items, such as video tapes or CDs. However, there are plenty of options for sectioning drawer interiors when necessary, including making wooden divisions in shapes and forms to partition and organize small or large objects.

Narrow desk drawers always benefit from a place to stash pens, pencils, or other small office items. You can make a classic pencil drawer by adding nothing more than a chunk of wood that's been coved on the shaper or tablesaw, attaching it at the front of the drawer with glue or nails.

BIG COVE HOLDS SMALL STUFF. A large cove cut into a blank of cherry provides a convenient spot for storing pens, pencils and other desk paraphernalia.

DIVIDER DOWELS. Thick wooden dowels, with 1/4-in.-dia. dowels glued into one end, fit into 1/4 in. holes drilled in a grid pattern through a piece of 3/4-in. plywood, which itself is screwed to the bottom of the drawer.

A

MEASURE, THEN NAIL. Glue and nail ¼-in.-thick strips of wood to opposite drawer sides. Use a combination square to ensure both strips are parallel.

B

A DRAWER WITHIN A DRAWER. Build a small drawer that rides on the strips, sizing it to be no more than half the parent drawer's depth to ensure easy access.

Another approach that works very well with large drawers is to screw or drop in a panel drilled with a series of holes into the bottom of the drawer, and then make a collection of dowels that fit into the holes. The idea is similar to trays seen in dishwashers. Install the dowels wherever you like to divide all sorts of large or odd-shaped items, such as kitchenware.

Drawer in a drawer

If your drawer is deep and tall enough, you can add another, smaller drawer that slides inside the big one. Be careful here, though: Plan on making the small drawer no bigger than half the parent drawer's depth, or you'll create an access problem.

1. Glue and nail wood strips to the sides of the parent drawer. **A**

2. Build a box to suit, dimensioning it to be just shy of the bigger drawer's width and no more that half its depth. **B**

Partitioning a drawer

No collection of drawers would be complete without traditional wooden dividers, or a set of thin wood strips that partition a drawer's interior for sorting and organizing all sorts of small gear. While you can buy high-quality dividers made from metals and plastics from many woodworking catalogs, it's just as easy to make your own. This system works best on relatively shallow drawers that are about 6 in. or less in height. Premium plywood that's ¼ in. thick, such as five-ply Baltic birch, makes an excellent material for dividers.

1. Start by lining the outer edges of the drawer with plywood strips fitted tight to the inside corners, rabbeting the corner joints for strength.

DADO BEGETS DADO. Line the exterior of the drawer first, and then start cutting dadoes in them to house more dividers. Place a divider into paired dadoes, and then use its position to mark for more dadoes.

EXTRA CUTS ADD VERSATILITY. If you cut extra dadoes, you can alter the division of the drawer without having to rework the dividers.

2. Divide the drawer by cutting dadoes into these outer parts, inserting a divider, and marking where more dadoes must be cut to create further divisions. **A** Keep your dadoes relatively shallow; $\frac{1}{16}$ in. deep in a $\frac{1}{4}$-in.-thick piece is about right. This keeps the dadoed part strong, an important feature since you're not going to glue the joint.

3. If your joinery went well, you should be able to slide the completed dividers into place without glue, and they'll stay put due to friction. This approach makes construction easier, and there's a bonus: If you need to reconfigure the drawer in the future, you can remove the parts, cut new dadoes, and make more dividers. For even more flexibility, you can cut more dadoes than you originally need, which lets you reconfigure the divisions on the fly. **B**

Lining a Drawer

Some drawers are made to hold delicate or precious objects. Unfortunately, the unforgiving wood sides of a typical drawer aren't particularly well suited for protecting certain valuables. To soften and cushion a drawer's interior, consider lining it with felt. You can buy it at fabric stores in a range of colors, and it's easy to apply inside a drawer.

1. Begin by measuring the interior of the drawer, then cut pieces of cardboard or matboard slightly undersized.

2. Cut each felt piece about 1 in. larger all around than the board, then cut the corners at roughly 45 degrees, so the felt runs slightly past the corners of the matboard.

3. Lay the board over the felt and spray a light coat of contact cement along the edges of the board and on the exposed felt. Then fold over the felt edges

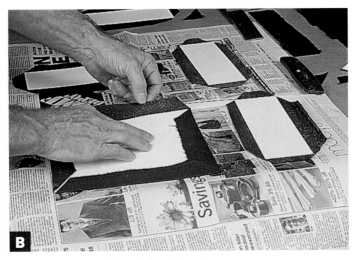

MITER AND FOLD THE EDGES. After mitering the corners of the felt, lay the board over it and spray the felt and the edges of the board with contact cement. Then wrap the felt around the edges of the board and press it in place.

onto the board and smooth out the joints with your hand. **A & B**

4. Squeeze a few beads of white or yellow glue over the backside of each liner, and then clamp the liner into the drawer. **C** Once the glue has dried, remove the clamps and fill the drawer with a few of your favorite things.

French-Fitting a Drawer

French-fitting a drawer, or cradling specific items in pockets in a box, drawer, or case, has a strong tradition that dates back several centuries for storing guns, artifacts, and other valued gear. It's still a great technique for housing modern treasures.

Although the technique here shows how to protect and cradle objects in a wooden pocket, traditional French-fitted drawers were covered in luxurious leather or velvet, adding a touch of class and an even higher level of protection. You can try your hand at this if you like, though the process is

ADD GLUE AND CLAMP. Run a bead of regular woodworking glue on the back of each panel, and then clamp it in the drawer using a block of wood to distribute clamp pressure.

tedious. Alternatively, you can use adhesive to stick felt to the pockets. Another option is to cover the interior with spray flocking, available from many woodworking catalogs.

1. Dimension a ½-in.-thick plywood panel to fit inside your drawer.

2. Lay out the intended contents as desired on the panel. Trace around each object with a pencil, adding semi-circles to create "lift pockets" for fingers. **A** After marking the board, you can refine each semi-circle using a compass or small round container like a film canister.

3. Use the scrollsaw to cut out the shapes, including the lift pockets. **B** You could drill a blade entry hole in each recess area, then thread the blade through to cut each individual hole, but that's not really necessary here. I prefer a more efficient approach: I enter the panel on one edge, and after cutting out the first shape, I make a straight cut to the next area, and so on. Exiting the blade out of the entry cut will keep the panel intact. The kerf that the scrollsaw blade leaves is so fine that you usually don't have to bother with gluing anything back together.

4. Use a chamfer bit in a small handheld router or in the router table to bevel all the sawn edges. You may need to touch up a few areas with a rasp or file to make acute corners and intersections more presentable.

5. Sand and finish the panel, lay it into the bottom of your drawer, and load it with your loot. **C**

LAY OUT AND TRACE. Position all the objects precisely where you want them, then trace around each with a pencil. Include semi-circular lift pockets to allow finger access.

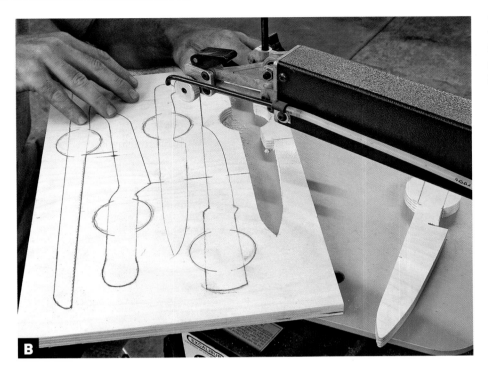

THIN BLADE LEAVES LITTLE TRACKS. Use the scrollsaw to cut the outlines of each shape. When done, exit the panel via your entry cut.

NESTED IN WOOD. Bevel the edges of the sawn areas with a chamfer bit to create more of a pillowed effect and to make it easier to access the lift pockets.

5 DESIGNING DOORS

- *Door Styles*
- *Door Anatomy*
- *Proportioning Doors*
- *Selecting Door Stock*
- *Choosing Hinges*

D oors are what we see when we look at a cabinet. Thanks to their relatively large surface area, they're the most visible component in a project, and they will make a lasting impression if you design them with this in mind. Like drawers, doors must function properly in addition to looking good. Opening and closing a door should be fluid and effortless. Sticky action, creaking hinges, or faulty catch mechanisms are not acceptable. A well-made door opens with little resistance, closes without clatter or fuss, and has a comfortable pull that fits the hand.

This part of the book will help you make doors with all these attributes—and more. Begin by choosing the style of door you want: overlay, half-overlay, or flush. After that, it's a design exercise in understanding wood movement, choosing the appropriate joinery, proportioning components carefully, selecting the right wood, buying and mounting the hinges, and adding a great finish. So let's open the world of doors and take a look inside!

Door Styles

As with drawer styles (see Chapter 1), there are three primary types of doors: overlay, half-overlay, and flush. Each style adds a different look and feel to the front of your cabinet, as well as offering some advantages and disadvantages.

Overlay doors are commonly seen in modern kitchens where, alongside overlay drawer fronts, they cover practically the entire face of the cabinets. The effect is sleek and seamless. The style works equally well in traditional furniture, as shown in the photo at right. Fitting this type of door takes some practice, as the gaps between adjacent doors or drawers must be exact, often within ⅛ in. or less.

Half-overlay doors, also called *lipped* doors, are typically used on cabinets that have face frames. The doors sit partially proud of the case, while their rabbeted edges allow them to rest slightly inside the case opening. Like a half-overlay drawer, this type of door is generally easier to fit, since the gap between the door and its opening is concealed and the space between adjacent doors and drawers is

SMOOTH AND SEAMLESS. Overlay doors work equally well on modern cabinets or traditional furniture, concealing the face of the case. Paired doors meet with a small reveal between them, and are flush with the case sides.

TYPES OF DOORS

Overlay

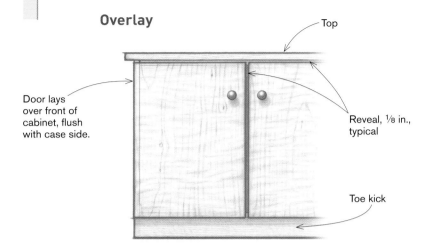

Top

Door lays over front of cabinet, flush with case side.

Reveal, 1/8 in., typical

Toe kick

Lipped or Half Overlay

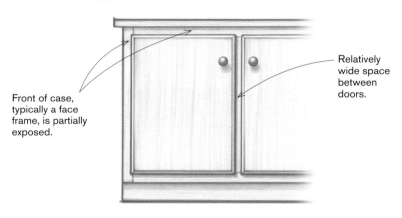
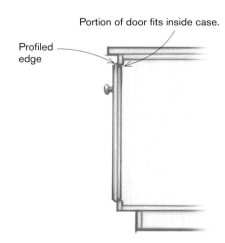

Portion of door fits inside case.

Profiled edge

Front of case, typically a face frame, is partially exposed.

Relatively wide space between doors.

Flush or Inset

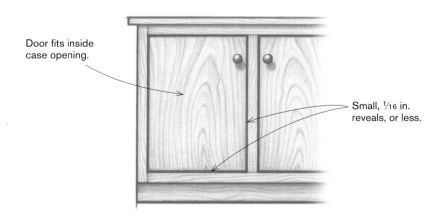

Door fits inside case opening.

Small, 1/16 in. reveals, or less.

Door is flush with face of case.

RABBET TO FIT. Lipped doors are often profiled or rounded on their edges, and lay over the case opening while a portion resides inside.

SMALL REVEALS ARE EXACT. Hung inside the case opening, flush doors require more precision during the fitting stage, but impart a more tailored look and feel.

work SMART

To simplify the installation of flush-fit doors, you can set them back slightly into the case where shadows will disguise any inconsistencies in the reveals, as seen with the bank of drawers on p. 73.

relatively large. A portion of the case or face frame is seen when using this style of door, so pay attention to the intended look on the front of your case during the design phase.

Flush doors, also called *inset* doors, require more attention during the fitting stage because the doors hang inside and level with the face of the case. To look good, this arrangement calls for very small reveals between the doors and case opening—often less than 1⁄16 in.—and a door face that's dead-flush to the case. Flush doors require a higher level of craftsmanship, but in truth are easier to fit than flush-fit drawers because there isn't all that fussy fitting deep inside the case. The look and feel of a well-made and properly-fitted flush door is satisfying—and worthy of an heirloom piece.

Door Anatomy

A typical cabinet door is made of *frame-and-panel* construction, in which a narrow, outer framework surrounds and captures a wide panel. (see the drawing on p. 100; I'll discuss slab-type doors in Chapter 6.)

The vertical frame pieces are called *stiles*, and the horizontal pieces are called *rails*. The frame is joined at the corners in a variety of ways, as I'll explain in Chapter 6. Typically, the stiles run full length and are mortised to receive tenons cut on the rails, though you can intentionally reverse this scenario for aesthetics or, in certain situations, for added strength. For example, on paired doors, rails that run the full width of the door add a visually unifying element, especially if you use continuous grain from rail to rail. You may also want to run rails full width to provide better screw purchase for hardware like knife hinges, which would otherwise be screwed into the end grain on the stiles.

DOOR ANATOMY

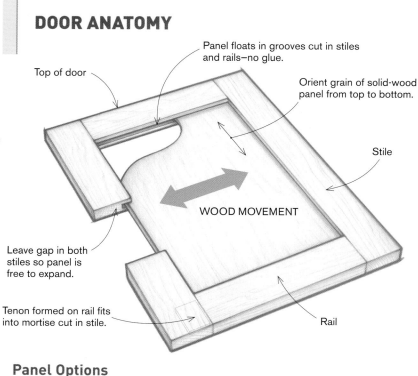

Panel floats in grooves cut in stiles and rails—no glue.

Top of door

Orient grain of solid-wood panel from top to bottom.

Stile

WOOD MOVEMENT

Leave gap in both stiles so panel is free to expand.

Tenon formed on rail fits into mortise cut in stile.

Rail

Panel Options

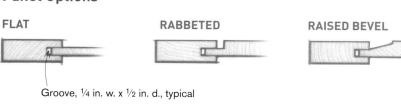

FLAT

RABBETED

RAISED BEVEL

Groove, ¼ in. w. x ½ in. d., typical

LET IT FLOW. Running the rails past the stiles works well with paired doors for a more harmonious look. Cut adjacent rails from a continuous piece of wood so the grain flows from door to door.

LONG GRAIN IS STRONGER. One reason to run door rails the full width of the door is to provide long-grain screw purchase for knife hinges. Otherwise, the screws would bite into the end-grain of the stiles, which is a weaker connection.

The stiles and rails house the panel, typically with a ½-in.-deep groove cut in the frame stock, though many router bit sets designed for door production produce a ⅜- or 7/16-in.-deep groove. Panels can be flat, rabbeted, or raised, either with a simple bevel or a raised bevel on one face. And it's up to you whether you install the panel with the rabbet or bevel facing outward, or whether you decide to display the flat face instead.

You can use either solid wood or plywood for panels, as I'll discuss in a bit. Typically, the grain on the panel runs vertically from top to bottom, but you can orient it across the face of the door if you wish to alter the look. If you're using a solid wood panel, you must allow room for seasonal expansion and contraction across the grain, as explained in the sidebar on the facing page.

CALCULATING SOLID WOOD PANEL MOVEMENT

Because wood movement is negligible along the grain, a solid wood panel can fit snugly between its top and bottom grooves. However, its width must accommodate seasonal movement across the grain. As a general guideline, expect most domestic North American woods to expand and contract between 1/8 in. and 1/4 in. per ft. of width throughout the year. The exact amount depends on species, type of cut, and geographic locale.

To calculate the panel width, first mill the frame grooves and joints, and dry-fit the frame. Then measure the panel opening, add the combined depth of the grooves, and subtract the expected amount of expansion. If you're building during the humid summer months, you can fit the panel tighter, as it will be shrinking more than swelling. If building during the dry winter months, allow for more swelling than shrinking.

JOINT IT NARROWER. After dimensioning the panel to fit its frame opening plus the depth of its grooves, remove about 1/8 in. from each long-grain edge.

GAPS ARE GOOD. Leaving a gap between the bottom of the frame grooves and the long-grain edges of the panel ensures the panel can expand across its width without busting the frame apart.

For an easy example, let's say you're building in a heated shop in January. Your project door has a 12-in.-wide opening and two 1/2-in.-deep grooves, which equals 13 in. Because it's the driest time of year, you'll want to allow for maximum expansion. Therefore, you might safely subtract a total of 1/4 in., yielding a panel width of 12 3/4 in.

If this math sounds confusing, relax. I find that taking the following approach works just fine for most average-size doors built throughout the year: I dry-fit the frame, measure the opening, add the total groove depth, and cut the panel to this dimension. Then I simply remove a total of about 1/4 in. from the long-grain edges by trimming 1/8 in. from each edge. You can do this on the tablesaw or with a few passes on the jointer. (Note: If you're rabbeting a panel, cut the rabbets after sizing the panel for wood movement.) Once you've glued up the door, a healthy gap should remain between the edge of the panel and the bottom of the groove.

Paired doors

Paired doors are common in furniture, offering easier access inside a case because of the larger opening they provide. You can build and hang them as you would a single door, letting them close with a small gap between them. A tidier look, however, and one that seals out dust, is achieved by designing the doors to close on each other. There are two approaches, but before you choose either, decide which door will open first, since the second door is captured until the first is opened.

The cleanest approach is to rabbet the edge of both doors so they nest together. Just remember to allow for some extra width on the innermost stile of the captured door, since it must project under the first door by the width of its rabbet. A ¼-in.-wide rabbet is usually sufficient for most cabinet doors. Oh, and if you forget to cut that one stile wider during the milling process? (I'm just sayin'.) No worries. Simply tack on a strip afterward with some brads and glue.

An easier method is to use an *astragal*, which is simply a strip of wood glued either to the face of the first door or attached to the back of the captured door. When you apply an astragal to the face, it becomes a visual element, so beveling its edges or contouring it with router bits is usually a good idea. If you opt for the more stealthy, behind-the-door approach, make sure to cut the astragal short so it won't interfere with any cabinet components, such as the case top or bottom.

OPPOSING RABBETS. Close the gap between paired doors by cutting matching rabbets in the edge of the stiles. Mill the depth of each rabbet to half the thickness of the door so the doors sit flush with each other when closed.

CLOSE IT WITH A STRIP. Nailing and gluing an astragal to the outside or inside of the door makes an effective dust-stopper. Remember to cut the strip short if it would interfere with any case components.

Proportioning Doors

Because doors are the primary focal point of a piece, it's important to proportion them so they'll work in harmony with each other as well as the drawers and other case components. Once you know the overall size of the cabinet and the style of door you'll be using, grab a scrap of paper and try sketching different sized doors to fit the case. Work out an arrangement that pleases your eye.

A frequent beginner's mistake is making doors and their case openings too tall or, more common, too wide. Wide doors are slower to open and require more swinging space. Plus, they put undue stress on the hinges. Tall doors suffer a similar fate, and, if they're narrow, they open too fast in an unexpected, herky-jerky movement. Small or narrow doors limit access into the cabinet behind them. Whenever possible, divide your case openings into reasonable sections, and build your doors to suit.

A few good rules of thumb: Limit door widths to 24 in. or less, and avoid building doors over 48 in. tall. Also, if the door is hinged (as opposed to a sliding door), don't make it wider than it is tall. If you need a particularly wide or tall opening in a case, use paired doors, or place one door above another. And if you must build an extra-wide or super-tall door, at least consider dividing up its framework by adding one or more intermediary stiles or rails to house two or more panels. The idea is to create harmony, balance, and a more detailed look. In this case, bigger isn't better, especially since a very wide panel may shrink enough to pull entirely away from its stile grooves.

As you dimension the various door parts, consider the width of the frame pieces. It's customary and quite acceptable to make the stiles and rails the same width. A width of 2½ to 3 in. is typical, and leaves enough room for mortising hinges and installing knobs, catches, and other hardware. However, you can add variety by using different widths in the same door. For example, try making the bottom rail a bit wider, say by an inch or so. A wider lower rail adds visual weight, which works particularly well when the door hangs below eye level, such as in a base cabinet.

Always keep the end result in mind: What will the cabinet look like once the doors are in place? If the case sides are a strong visual element at the front of the cabinet, consider narrowing the outer door stiles so they appear as one with the case sides. In the same vein, with paired doors you may want to incorporate smaller inner stiles so the area where they meet doesn't become too visually heavy. Designing a door is your chance to have fun, so take the plunge and try something new.

GOOD PROPORTIONS

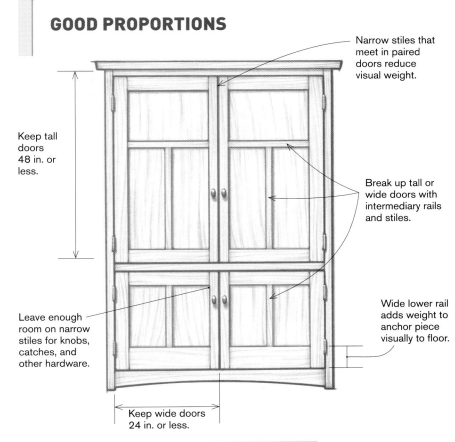

Narrow stiles that meet in paired doors reduce visual weight.

Keep tall doors 48 in. or less.

Break up tall or wide doors with intermediary rails and stiles.

Leave enough room on narrow stiles for knobs, catches, and other hardware.

Wide lower rail adds weight to anchor piece visually to floor.

Keep wide doors 24 in. or less.

SLENDER CENTER. Furniture maker Gary van Rawlins strikes a better balance on these wenge and tulipwood doors by using narrower stiles where they meet in the middle.

Selecting Door Stock

Doors dress up the front of a cabinet, which is reason enough to choose your stock carefully. But there's more at stake. Selecting the right wood will help your doors survive daily wear and tear and, if you're lucky, generations of satisfied use.

Manmade panels, such as plywood and MDF, are excellent choices for doors, particularly if you're making a slab-type door or choosing stock for panels. But for frames, clear, straight-grained hardwood is generally your best bet.

Solid wood

Whether you're making a full-width slab door or building frame-and-panel construction, the same applies: Solid wood doors have an authentic feel.

If you're making frame-and-panel doors, bear in mind that it's the frame that keeps a door flat because it prevents the panel from cupping. Mill your frame stock ¾ in. to 1 in. thick for strength, and keep frame pieces relatively narrow—about

4 in., or less—so that wood movement is minimized. Use clear, quartered or riftsawn stock if you can. A neat trick is to get this straight-grained stuff from wider plainsawn boards by ripping material from the edges, as shown in the bottom left photo.

When it comes to panels, I always try to use full-width boards whenever possible, because it's a chance to express the tree's natural growth and beauty. However, wide boards are hard to come by. Thankfully, narrow stock will do nicely if you edge-glue it together, cutting your stock from the same board so that grain, color, and texture are a good match in the panel.

Mill your panels to a thickness that works well with the frame and the cabinet. A ¾-in.-thick panel is typical and adds a desirable stoutness, but it will often project beyond a ¾-in.-thick frame. Depending on your design, this can sometimes look bulky from the front or interfere with case parts inside. Thinner, ¼-in. panels are fine for small doors but, like drawer bottoms that are too thin, they often cheapen the feel of a standard-size door and

RIFT FROM PLAIN. Sawing stock from the edges of a plain-sawn board renders straight-grained, riftsawn material—a great way to get stable frame stock.

WIDER WOOD. Make a wide panel from a narrow board by jointing the edges of two or more boards, and then gluing them together with clamps.

sound flimsy when the door is closed against the case. A door with a ½-in.-thick panel is just about right, offering sufficient thickness so it can be rabbeted to sit flush with the frame or set back without obstructing interior case fittings. The same applies to plywood panels.

Plywood and veneer

As modern woodworkers, we're lucky to have sheet goods available to us. Hardwood-veneer plywood comes in a variety of tasty species in an endless array of colors, grain patterns, and textures. This can really add spice to a door, particularly when used as panel stock in a frame-and-panel door.

Premium plywood and MDF are also excellent choices for panels, and make a great base for adding your own veneer. Remember that plywood can be glued into the frame grooves to strengthen the entire door.

Another approach is to use manmade panels for paint-grade doors. MDF is particularly good for

this, with its smooth, ready-to-paint surface. Since wood movement isn't an issue, not only can you glue the panel into the frame, but you can add decorative touches, such as applying molding directly to the door.

SHOP-VENEERED PANEL. Premium-grade plywood can be covered with your favorite veneer and rabbeted to expose its raw edges. Gluing the panel into the frame strengthens the entire door.

READY FOR PAINT. A popular frame, MDF panel, and wood molding nailed and glued to the panel makes a sturdy, paint-grade door without worries of wood movement.

TYPES OF HINGES

Butt

Use for overlay and flush.

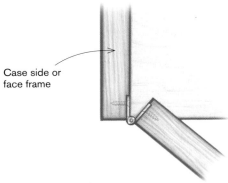

Case side or face frame

No-Mortise Butt

Use for overlay and flush.

Leaf on door rests inside or to the side of case leaf.

Knife

Use for overlay and flush.

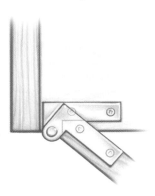

Surface Mount

Use for overlay, half overlay, and flush.

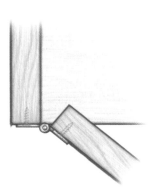

Leaf offset for half overlay.

Barrel

Use for bi-fold, overlay, and flush.

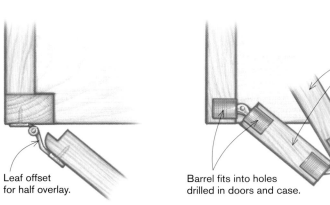

Bi-fold doors

Barrel fits into holes drilled in doors and case.

Continuous

Use for overlay and flush.

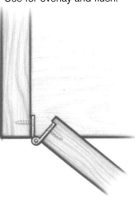

Cup

Use for overlay, half overlay, and flush.

Cup fits into hole drilled in door; base plate screwed to case.

PICK YOUR SWING. Hinges come in many styles, and in different sizes, materials, and finish. Clockwise from top: butt, no-mortise butt, knife, surface-mount, barrel, continuous, and cup.

Choosing Hinges

A sweet, smooth-acting door is directly related to its hinges, so it pays to get the best. Look for solid castings or extrusions (which are sturdier than the stamped variety), thick hinge plates, called leaves, and precision-made barrels, or knuckles, that pivot smoothly without play. Buying a good hinge is only half the battle. Some hinges can be used interchangeably for flush, half-overlay, and overlay doors; others cannot. There are many styles to choose from, so it's important to select the correct hinge before committing to its installation. (See Chapter 7 for more on installing hinges.)

You'll also want to consider what you'll see on the outside of the cabinet once the door is hinged. At one end of the spectrum is the surface-mounted hinge, which puts both leaves and knuckle on prominent display. To downplay your hinges, you can install an inconspicuous knife hinge, which reveals a button-sized barrel and little else. For a hardware-free look on the outside, barrel and cup hinges are a good option. A furniture maker's standard, the ubiquitous butt hinge is readily available in a range of sizes, materials, and finishes, and strikes a good balance between ease of installation, sturdy action, and good looks.

AN OLD STANDBY. Butt hinges are straightforward to install. They support small or large doors, and reveal a distinctive barrel that projects from the door and case.

6 BUILDING DOORS

B uilding doors involves first choosing and constructing the cabinet where they will live, then selecting and cutting appropriate door joints and putting together fully assembled, ready-to-mount doors. The information in this chapter is designed to help you do just that, and to generate some fine doors while expanding your door-building prowess.

For doors with frames, the corner joints are key to the overall strength of the door, so it's important to choose the appropriate joints for the type of door you're building. The mortise-and-tenon is a standard joint for frames, but there are several other options. You can always choose a solid panel instead, which is often much simpler to build than a frame and might better harmonize with the cabinet you're making. And don't forget glass doors. They can add drama to an otherwise plain-looking door, and the simple versions are easy to build.

Building a Case for Doors

You have two basic choices when attaching doors to a cabinet. You can hang them on the case itself or on a face frame that's attached to the case. When hung on the case, a door can screw to the case sides, dividers, or to the top and bottom. As you design and build your cabinet, remember that the type of door and its hinges have as much impact on the design as the type of door construction. So be sure to decide first on the hinging system and door style, whether overlay, half-overlay, or inset.

If you build a case with a projecting top and bottom, you can hinge the door to these surfaces instead of the sides. One option, which makes the door look cradled by the cabinet, is to rabbet the sides of the case and then hang the door on knife hinges mortised into the case top and bottom, with the door recessed slightly in the rabbet (see the top right photo on p. 111).

Instead of hinges, you can opt for doors that slide on tracks. (For more on building sliding doors, see Chapter 8.) The only critical requirement when building the case is to leave enough depth at the

HIDDEN INSIDE. On cabinets without frames, side walls and dividers hold the door. These particular cup hinges require wood blocks glued to the case to align the door correctly.

CASES AND FRAMES FOR DOORS

Face Frame

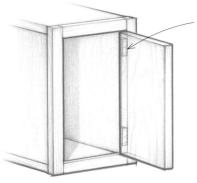

Attach butt hinge to edge of frame and edge of door.

Frameless

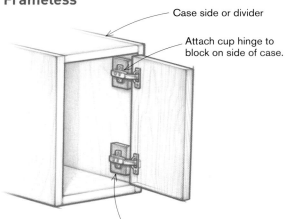

Case side or divider

Attach cup hinge to block on side of case.

If necessary, glue block of wood to case side to align door.

Frameless with Projecting Top and Bottom

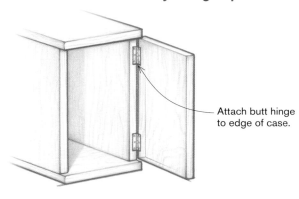

Attach butt hinge to edge of case.

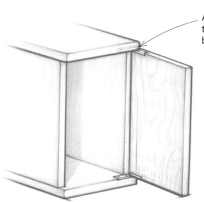

Attach knife hinge to case top and bottom.

Case for Sliding Doors

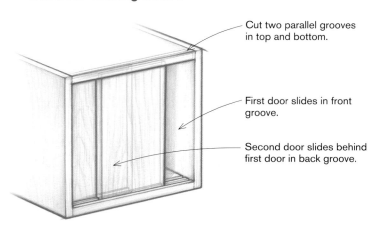

Cut two parallel grooves in top and bottom.

First door slides in front groove.

Second door slides behind first door in back groove.

SCREWED TO THE FACE. This flush door hangs on butt hinges screwed into the face frame on a traditional case.

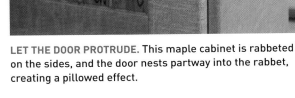

LET THE DOOR PROTRUDE. This maple cabinet is rabbeted on the sides, and the door nests partway into the rabbet, creating a pillowed effect.

front for the tracks that guide the doors. This usually means setting back shelves, partitions, and the like (see the drawing on the facing page).

Just as you would with drawers, build the case before you start milling door parts. Once you have the cabinet assembled, use the case openings to determine the size of the doors.

Choosing Door Joints

Door joinery falls into two basic categories: joints for slab (solid) doors, and joints for frame-and-panel doors. While there are various types of slab doors, joinery is straightforward and usually consists of bracing on the back or ends of the door to keep the panel flat, as I'll explain in detail later in this chapter. On the other hand, frame-and-panel doors get their strength from the corner joints in the frame, and there are several choices available to the woodworker (see the drawing on p. 112).

The panel in a frame-and-panel door fits into grooves cut in the frame, typically ¼ in. wide by ½ in. deep. The grooves—just like those cut in drawer sides to accept a drawer bottom (see Chapter 2)—can be cut with a router, or by using a dado blade on the tablesaw. Stopped grooves must be routed. Aim for a sliding fit of the panel in the groove, so it's free to move a bit to accommodate seasonal expansion and contraction.

When it comes to joining frame corners, there's no substitute for the time-honored mortise-and-tenon joint. Although you can use biscuits or dowels, a mortise-and-tenon joint is the standard by which all other joints are measured because of its superior strength and long-term durability in door frames.

When designing your joints, make your mortises as deep as possible for the greatest strength. Make your tenons about ¹⁄₁₆ in. shy of the mortise depth to ensure that the tenon shoulders make good contact with the mortised piece. In an average cabinet door,

CORNER JOINTS

Blind Mortise and Tenon

Panel floats in grooves in frame.

Stop groove in stiles.

Groove for panel, ¼ in. wide x ½ in. deep, typical

Stile

Rail

Tenon cut in rail glued into mortise cut in stile.

Through Tenon

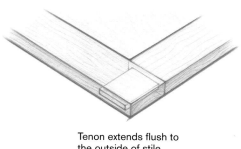

Tenon extends flush to the outside of stile.

Haunched Tenon

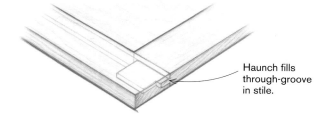

Haunch fills through-groove in stile.

Floating Tenon

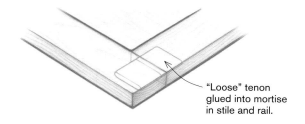

"Loose" tenon glued into mortise in stile and rail.

Biscuits or Dowels

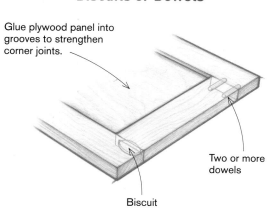

Glue plywood panel into grooves to strengthen corner joints.

Two or more dowels

Biscuit

Cope and Stick

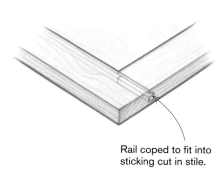

Rail coped to fit into sticking cut in stile.

Miter with Through Tenon

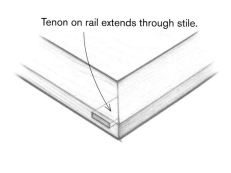

Tenon on rail extends through stile.

TWO ARE BETTER THAN ONE. Join wide rails with two or more tenons housed in separate mortises to avoid problems with wood movement.

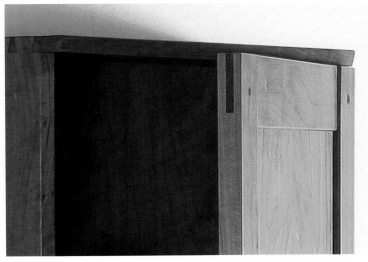

ALL THE WAY THROUGH. A bridle joint is easy to make because the open mortise can be sawn on the tablesaw. The darker end grain of the tenon reveals itself on the edge of the door for a classic look.

I strive to make my mortise-and-tenons joints at least 1¼ in. deep.

Keep in mind that if you're joining wide rails, you'll want to avoid tenons wider than about 4 in. to minimize wood movement problems. One solution is to divide wide tenons into narrower ones, which is easily done by first milling a single tenon and then splitting it into multiple tenons on the bandsaw.

You can also use a bridle joint, which is a variety of mortise-and-tenon joint. It's common in door joinery and great for the small shop because you can cut both the mortise and the tenon with just a few simple setups on the tablesaw—with no mortising bits required.

Another alternative is to use floating, or "loose," tenons. Here, you mortise both the stile and the rail with a slot mortiser or a plunge router equipped with an edge guide, and then join the pieces with a separate tenon that's sized to fit the mortises. One of the benefits with this approach is that there's less confusion when dimensioning the rails because you don't have to take into account the extra length for the tenons. Plus, it's easy to get the tenon to fit

precisely since, as a separate piece of wood, it's a snap to send it through the thickness planer (oversized in length, of course) or sneak up on the final fit with a hand plane.

MORTISE RAILS AND STILES. Loose tenons simplify the task of dimensioning parts, and are just as strong as integral tenons. Cut shallow grooves on the tenon cheeks to allow air and glue to escape during assembly.

Making Mortise-and-Tenon Joints

There are many ways to cut a mortise and the tenon that fits it. Regardless of your tooling, always cut the mortise first, as it's much easier to adjust a tenon to fit a mortise than the other way around. Also, when calculating the length of door rail stock, don't forget to include the combined length of the two tenons.

Cutting a mortise

Cutting mortises can be a struggle for a small-shop woodworker. One approach is to drill out the majority of the waste by hand and then chisel to your layout lines. However, using power tools greatly speeds up the process. A hollow-chisel mortiser is a wise investment, and produces a clean, square-ended mortise if you follow the correct cutting sequence, which is to cut the outside shoulders

MORTISE WITH A HOLLOW CHISEL. Define the square shoulders at the ends of the mortise first, and then chisel the area between by taking a series of overlapping cuts.

work SMART

There is an optimum "slip-fit" to a well-made mortise-and-tenon joint. As a woodworking mentor once noted, "It shouldn't be so tight that you have to beat it together with a hammer. On the other hand, it shouldn't be so loose that you can tap it home with your hat."

ROUT A MORTISE. Clamp a wide board to the bench to steady the router, and use a plunge router equipped with a mortising bit and edge guide to cut a super-clean, round-ended mortise.

SAW IT UPRIGHT. Commercial or shop-made tenoning jigs do a great job of sawing the cheeks. To speed up the process, use two rip blades with a wood spacer between them to cut both cheeks in one pass.

first, then cut the waste between the shoulders by making a series of overlapping cuts.

If you have a plunge router, you can rout a mortise using a mortising bit and an edge guide. Clamp the work to your bench, with its edge aligned to a wide, thick piece of dressed stock to help support the router. Remember that routed mortises will have rounded ends produced by the bit. You can square them up either with a chisel to fit a standard square tenon or round the tenon to fit, as I'll describe in a moment.

Sawing a tenon

Tenons can be made by hand with a backsaw or framesaw, cutting carefully to your layout lines.

Again, power tools make the job a snap. The tablesaw is typically the weapon of choice, with many woodworkers using a commercial or shop-made tenoning jig to support the work on end for cutting the tenon cheeks. Once the cheeks are cut, lay the work flat on the saw, guiding it with the miter gauge to cut the tenon shoulders.

I prefer the convenience of cutting tenons with a dado blade. I set the tablesaw rip fence to establish the desired tenon length, and then saw the tenons using two different blade-height setups without changing the rip fence setting. The first series of passes cuts the cheeks and wide shoulders by laying the stock first on one face, then flipping it over to cut the opposing cheek and wide shoulder. The

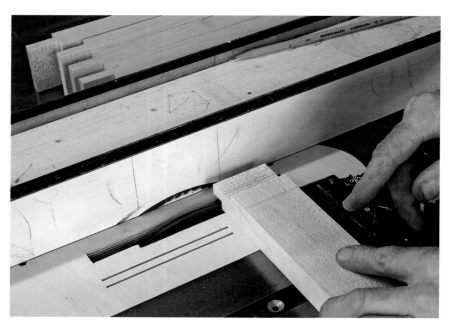
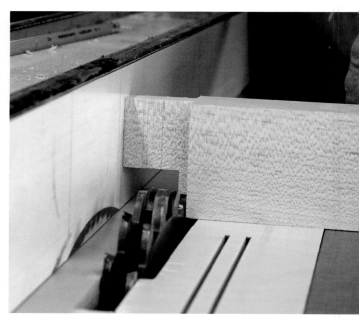

SAW IT HORIZONTAL. A dado blade makes quick work of cutting a tenon. Make a series of overlapping cuts to saw the cheeks and wide shoulders, then reset the blade height and cut the narrow shoulders feeding the stock on edge.

ROUNDING A TENON. Make a few chisel cuts at the shoulder, then round the edges of the tenon with arcing strokes from a rasp. The fit doesn't need to be perfect; just file until the joint goes together.

second series of cuts is made feeding the stock on edge to create the narrow shoulders. When taking this "flip-the-stock" approach, it's critical that your mortises be accurately centered across the thickness of the stock when the door frame pieces are the same thickness.

If you're lucky, your joint will fit as intended. However, if you overcut the tenon, you can glue and clamp some veneer to one or both cheeks to fatten it up a bit. On the other hand, the tenon may be a bit fat and need some thinning, either by planing the cheeks with a shoulder plane or by carefully filing with a patternmaker's rasp, which leaves a much smoother surface than your run-of-the-mill rasp. If you're fitting the tenon to a round-ended mortise, use a rasp or chisel to round over the edges. You can also use sandpaper wrapped around a hardwood block, but be careful not to damage the tenon shoulder.

ALIGNING CLAMPS

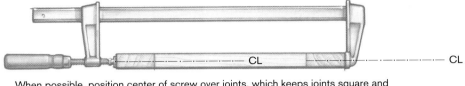

When possible, position center of screw over joints, which keeps joints square and assembly flat.

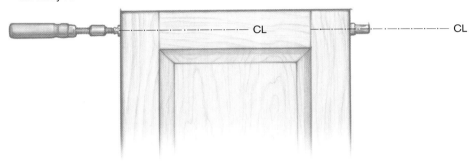

Door Assembly

Once you've grooved the frame, cut the corner joints, and shaped a panel to fit, you're ready for assembly. If you're building a door with a solid-wood panel, be careful to keep glue out of the grooves and away from the panel so it can expand and contract in the frame without binding. Use moderate clamp pressure to bring your joints home, and before you set a door aside to dry, make sure it's square.

Take care not to introduce twist during clamp-up. To ensure your door goes together flat, work on a flat surface, and orient the clamps so they're in line with the joints and the plane of the door, as shown in the drawing above. Once you've aligned the clamps, use gentle pressure—just enough to close the joints.

SQUARE IT BEFORE IT DRIES. Compare the two diagonals on the clamped-up door to check for square. If one side is longer, offset the clamps in that direction to nudge the door into square.

BRADS BECOME CLAMPS. After clamping up a door, you can use a brad nailer on the backside to secure the joint near the shoulder, which frees up your clamps for the next glue-up.

Pinning and Pegging Joints

Pegs highlight the joints in a frame, and can save time when it comes to clamping doors. Keep in mind that in most situations a pegged joint won't strengthen the connection. However, if the glue does fail at some point in the future, at least the peg will keep things together.

Pins and dowels

Pins and brads, especially when shot with a pneumatic gun, offer a quick way to keep a joint together while the glue dries. If you're in a hurry, or you're assembling a boatload of doors and don't have a fleet of clamps at your disposal, clamp a door together and then pin the joints from the backside.

PIN IT WITH BAMBOO. Drill through the joint with a brad-point bit, glue and tap in a bamboo skewer, and then cut it level with a flush-cutting saw.

This approach lets you remove the clamps right away and start working on another door.

A standard ¼-in.-dia. hardwood dowel from the hardware store makes great peg material, but I find it a bit commonplace and overly heavy for pegging joints. I recommend using the incredibly tough and resilient ⅛-in.-dia. bamboo skewers commonly available from the grocery store, or ³⁄₁₆-in. bamboo chopsticks from your favorite restaurant. Chuck a ⅛-in.- or ³⁄₁₆-in.-dia. brad-point bit in your drill, and drill a skewer hole through the joint, using a back-up block on the exit side to minimize tear-out. Brush the dowel with glue, tap it into the hole, and cut it level to the surface with a flush-cutting saw.

Square pegs

Instead of dowels, you can use square stock to peg your joints. One method is to drill a round hole and then hammer the square stock into a hole that's about ¹⁄₃₂ in. oversize. This works particularly well if you're working with soft to medium-hard woods,

such as pine, cherry, or walnut, as the round hole deforms a bit as the peg is driven in. For added flair, you can orient the peg diagonally to create a diamond effect when it's installed.

If you want very precise-looking square pegs, you'll first need to create square holes into which they'll fit. You can use a hollow-chisel mortiser to cut the holes, or drill them out and then square them up carefully with a narrow chisel. For added zest, chisel small chamfers on the edges of the hole, highlighting the corners with deep miter cuts, and bevel the end of the peg. If your corner joint is big enough, try using two or more pegs, and vary their size for maximum effect.

Slab Doors

The simplest door you can build is a slab door, made from a single piece of wood or plywood. Plywood is your easiest option because there's no wood movement to contend with. Solid-wood panels need more engineering to keep them flat and to prevent warp.

DOUBLE YOUR FUN. On large joints, you can use two different sized pegs to add interest. Epoxy holds the pegs in place, but be sure to wipe off any excess before it sets.

TOP AND BOTTOM FIRST. Glue and clamp the top and bottom banding first to conceal the plywood edges. Inset the strips slightly on one edge of the door in preparation for the next step.

SIDE STRIPS ARE NEXT. Glue the side strips in place, again using cauls and letting the banding overhang the top and bottom of the door.

PLANE IT LIKE WOOD. After trimming the banding flush at the corners and smooth on both faces, you can work the edges just like solid wood. A few swipes with a block plane create a pleasing chamfer.

Plywood panel

A plywood slab door is quick to make. The only real work is concealing the raw edges. One easy approach is to cover them with veneer edging, sometimes called "veneer tape." It is sold in rolls with a hot-melt adhesive on the backside, allowing you to press it onto the edges of the door with a hot iron. However, this thin edging is best reserved for utility or lower-end doors because it's not particularly durable. A better option is to add solid wood "banding," which is simply thin strips of wood glued to the edges of the door.

To make the banding, I typically rip strips between ⅛ in. and 3/16 in. thick, which allows me to round over lightly or chamfer the edges later, much as I would with solid wood. Mill the strips to be slightly wider than your plywood is thick so you can plane, scrape, or sand the edging flush with the panel after application. If you plan to cut a more complex profile on the edges of the door, simply make your strips thicker.

1. Cut the panel to length, accounting for the thickness of the banding, but keeping the panel a little oversized in width for now.

2. Glue and clamp the banding to the top and bottom of the door, avoiding overhang on one edge and using wide cauls to distribute clamping pressure. **A**

3. Once the glue has dried, place the panel edge without the overhang against your rip fence and trim the banding on the opposite edge flush with the panel. Then trim the opposite edge flush, bringing the door to final width minus the thickness of the two side bandings to come.

4. Add the side banding as you did the first two strips, this time letting them overhang both the top and bottom edges. **B**

5. When the glue is dry, trim the overhang flush at each corner, then level the banding with the front and back of the panel, and soften the edges by rounding or beveling them with a router bit or a plane. **C**

Solid-wood panel

A solid wood slab door is a different animal altogether. You must provide some method of bracing the panel to prevent warping. A simple, tried-and-true method is to add bracing, or battens, to the back of the door. This type of door is known as a board-and-batten door, and can sport a pair of horizontal battens, three battens in the shape of a "Z," or any number of configurations that help keep the panel flat. Just screw the battens to the back of the door, and you're done. (Don't glue the battens, or you'll create a cross-grain problem.)

BRACED AT THE BACK. Nail or screw two or more wood cleats, called *battens*, to the back of a solid panel to keep it flat over time.

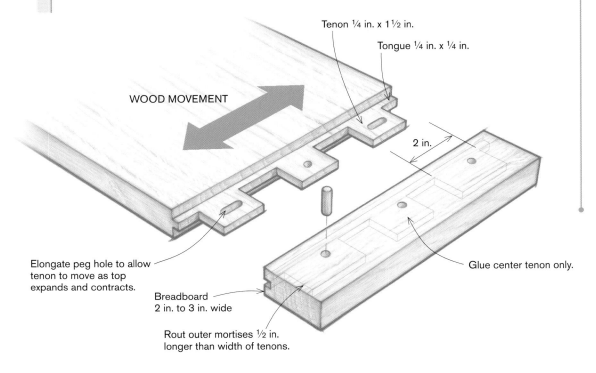

BREADBOARD CONSTRUCTION

WOOD MOVEMENT

Tenon ¼ in. x 1½ in.

Tongue ¼ in. x ¼ in.

2 in.

Glue center tenon only.

Elongate peg hole to allow tenon to move as top expands and contracts.

Breadboard 2 in. to 3 in. wide

Rout outer mortises ½ in. longer than width of tenons.

work **SMART**

Board-and-batten doors were traditionally braced on the back with cleats held by clenched nails. To clench a nail, it must protrude an inch or so from the back of the door, after which you bend just the tip using a pliers or small anvil. Hammer down the protruding section of the nail so that the bent tip reenters the wood. The technique may sound somewhat crude, but it remains a very effective method for joining battens to the back of a door.

A more complex slab door is one that incorporates breadboard ends, which are narrow boards that run across the ends of the panel to keep it flat. Construction must be done carefully to prevent cross-grain wood-movement problems.

1. Start by preparing the panel and the breadboards. Leave the breadboards oversized in length for now, and saw or rout a ¼-in.-deep groove into one edge of each breadboard.

2. Cut a single full-length tenon on each end of the panel. Dry-fit each breadboard end onto the tenon, and lay out three individual tenons and mortises (or more if the panel is extra wide). Aim for a snug fit side-to-side on the central tenon, and leave ⅛ in. to ¼ in. of space on each side of each outer tenon, depending on the species you're using and the width of the panel. **A**

3. Cut the ¼-in.-wide by 1¼-in.-deep (or deeper) mortises in each breadboard end.

4. Saw out the individual tenons on the panel with a jigsaw or on the bandsaw, leaving a ¼-in.-long tongue between each tenon. **B**

5. Dry-assemble the breadboard and drill peg holes through the assembly at each tenon. Then disassemble the parts and elongate the peg holes on the

ROOM TO MOVE. With the panel tenon sitting in the breadboard groove, lay out the mortises and tenons, leaving extra space for wood movement at the outer tenons.

LEAVE THE TONGUE. Saw the individual tenons to width, leaving a ¼-in. tongue in between.

ENLARGE THE HOLES. Use a straightedge and a straight bit to elongate the peg holes in the outer tenons.

GLUE THE MIDDLE. Brush glue onto the center tenon and mortise only, then assemble the breadboard with clamps and pin the joint with the pegs.

outermost tenons. You can do this with a coping saw or a chisel, but I prefer to set up a straightedge and follow that with a straight bit and a router. **C** At this point, cut the breadboard to finished length.

6. Assemble the breadboards to the door by applying glue to the center tenon and mortise only. **D** Clamp the parts together, and then drive the pegs through the joints. **E** The completed door is stable and ready for hinging. As the wood swells and shrinks, the panel and its outer tenons are free to move along the elongated holes without sacrificing strength. **F**

work SMART

To accentuate the joints and hide imperfections, I like to plane and chisel small chamfers on all the shoulders of a breadboard joint before assembly. When the parts come together, the mating chamfers create small V-shaped grooves, which add a distinct shadow line while disguising any small misalignments.

FLAT FOREVER. Ready for hinging, this breadboard door will survive many seasons of wood movement without warping.

GROOVE, THEN MORTISE. After plowing through-grooves in all the frame parts, cut a mortise ½ in. in from each end of each stile.

A

B

HAUNCH FILLS GAP. When cutting the outside shoulder in the rail, leave a ½ in. haunch to fill the groove in the stile.

C

END-GRAIN FIRST. Rout the bevel with the stock face down, starting with one end-grain edge and then rotating the panel in sequence to reduce tear-out.

Frame-and-Panel Doors

Arguably the most prevalent of all doors, the traditional frame-and-panel has been around for a long time, and for good reason. By capturing a solid-wood panel in grooves in a relatively narrow frame, the problem of wood movement on wide, solid panels is solved. The panel is free to move in the grooves, while the frame keeps the panel flat. Thanks, woodworking forebears!

Although there are nuances with the joinery and panel style, the following construction is a good example of this kind of door.

1. Start by grooving the frame stock for the panel, and then cut the mortises in the stiles, insetting them ½ in. in from the ends of the stock and aligning them with the panel groove. **A**

2. Since the groove is cut all the way through, cut a haunched tenon to fill the gap at the end of the stiles. **B** Test-fit the joints, adjusting the tenons as necessary with a shoulder plane or rasp until you achieve a slip fit into the mortises.

3. Cut the panel to size and shape its edges to fit the grooves in the frame. (For more on sizing panels, see Door Anatomy, Chapter 5.) Set up a raised-panel cutter in the shaper or router table, and bevel one end-grain edge first. Follow this by shaping the

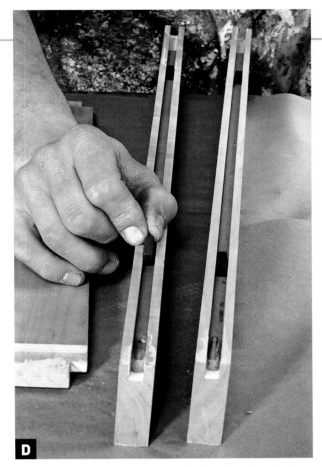

ONLY THE MORTISES AND TENONS. Spread glue onto the tenons and into the mortises, keeping a watchful eye that glue doesn't stray into the panel grooves.

GENTLE, BUT FIRM. Use firm pressure from the clamps to close the joints, but don't overdo it.

RUBBER STOPS RATTLE. Drop a pair of anti-rattle strips into each stile groove before you assemble the door to keep the panel from shifting sideways or rattling during the seasons.

adjacent long-grain edge to remove any tear-out from the previous cut. **C** Follow the same routing sequence to bevel the remaining two sides.

4. You're ready for assembly. Before you put the parts together, place a few spacers in the grooves of the stile pieces. Known by various trade names, such as Panalign Strips® or Spaceballs®, these compressible strips or balls of synthetic rubber keep the panel centered and prevent it from rattling during the dry season. **D**

Slip the panel between two rails, and apply glue into the stile mortises and on the tenons, being careful not to let it run into the frame grooves. **E** Be mindful here: If any glue escapes into the grooves, it will lock the panel in place and defeat the free-floating nature of the panel, possibly cracking it

later. Once the joints are closed, lightly clamp across them, check the door for square, and set it aside on a flat surface to dry. **F**

work SMART

If you don't have a router table or a raised-panel cutter, you can easily raise a door panel on the tablesaw with the blade tilted to the desired angle, using the same approach as you would for a beveled drawer bottom (see "Adding the bottom", on p. 39).

PRE-STAINING PANELS

If you plan to stain your doors, it's wise to pre-color the edges of solid wood panels before assembly. This way, when the panel shrinks due to seasonal changes, it won't expose unstained wood. An easy approach is to stain the long-grain edges using a foam brush that has been notched to indicate the depth of the panel groove.

COLOR BEFORE ASSEMBLY. Use a foam brush to stain the long-grain edges of the panel before assembly to prevent exposing unstained wood when it inevitably shrinks.

GLUE IT ALL. You can size a plywood panel to seat fully in its panel grooves. For the greatest strength, apply glue into the grooves, then clamp up the door.

Quick and Strong Door

Sometimes the best door is the one that's quickest to make. Thanks to a few simple machine setups and a plywood panel, you'll be hanging this door in no time.

The joinery is based on a stub tenon and a plywood panel that you glue into the frame. Essentially, the panel holds the door joints together, so a ½-in.-long stub tenon is sufficient for the frame corners. Alternatively, you could join the frame with biscuits after routing stopped panel grooves in the stiles.

1. Cut through-grooves in all the frame pieces.

2. Mill stub tenons to fit the grooves.

3. Make a plywood panel, in this case sizing it to seat fully in the grooves.

4. Spread a generous amount of glue into the grooves and onto the stub tenons, then clamp up the door. **A**

READY FOR PAINT.
MDF can be glued into the frame grooves just like plywood. Because the cut surfaces of MDF are extremely porous, it's a good idea to prime them before assembly.

If you're making a door that's going to be painted, you can choose MDF to create a raised panel instead of a flat panel. The same rules apply: Since the panel is dimensionally stable, you can use only stub tenons and glue the edges of the panel into the frame. **B**

Cope-and-Stick Door

Popular with the kitchen cabinetmaking industry, the cope-and-stick door can be produced quickly and efficiently, and it offers a complex profile that surrounds the panel for added visual appeal. While the industry uses large shapers and specialized cutters to produce this type of joint, the small shop can take advantage of router bits made expressly for this purpose. There are many types of bits to choose from, including one-piece cutters or matched sets, and they're available in various profiles, ranging from a simple thumbnail to more intricate ogee shapes. However, they all work along the same principle: The ends of the door rails are coped to

MATCHED SET. The sticking bit (left) creates the profile along the inner edge of the frame pieces, while the coping bit (right) shapes the ends of the rails to fit the sticking.

BEEFING UP COPE-AND-STICK

Cabinet manufacturers routinely market cabinet doors whose frame strength relies solely on the ½-in.-long stub tenon that is an integral part of cope-and-stick joinery. It's normal for these joints to fail, as shown in the photo at right. As woodworkers, we can do better. You can reinforce a cope-and-stick joint with a pair of dowels but, for maximum strength, I suggest adding a floating tenon instead. Correctly fitted, a hardwood loose tenon is as strong as a conventional mortise-and-tenon joint, and is often easier to construct for the small-shop woodworker.

NOT MUCH THERE. This cope-and-stick door joint failed in use. The torn fibers reveal just how little held the joint together in the first place.

TENONS CAN COPE. Gluing a loose tenon into mating mortises cut in the stiles and rails significantly strengthens a cope-and-stick joint. An unreinforced joint is shown underneath for comparison.

match the sticking profile cut along the inner edge of the frame.

Although there is a fair amount of gluing surface with this joint, I would caution you to reinforce the connection by either using a plywood panel and gluing it into the grooves, or strengthening the joint with dowels or tenons (see the sidebar above).

With the matched router bit set shown here, the stock is placed face down on the router table to make all the cuts.

1. Install the sticking bit in the table, and rout the stiles and rails, using a hold-down and a pushstick for accuracy and safety. **A** Working with rail stock that's oversized in width makes for safer handling during the next step.

2. Install the coping bit in the table, and adjust it to the correct height by aligning it with the sticking in one of the frame pieces. **B** Cope a piece of extra frame stock along one long edge. You'll nest this piece into the profiled edge of your rail stock to

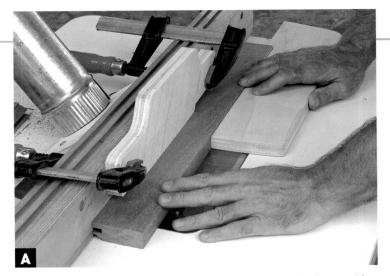

A

STICK AND GROOVE. Rout the sticking and cut the groove for the panel in one pass, using a notched pushstick to guide the narrow stiles.

B

GAUGE THE HEIGHT. Use one of the sticking pieces to set the height of the coping bit, aligning the cutters on the bit so they're level with their mating cuts on the piece.

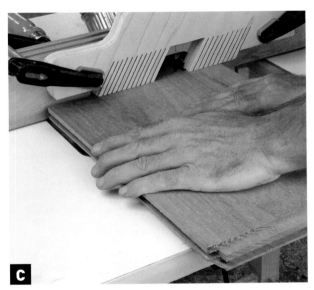

C

COPE LIKE THIS. Rout the coped profile in the ends of the oversized rail stock. To prevent exit tear-out, back up the cut with a scrap piece of coped stock.

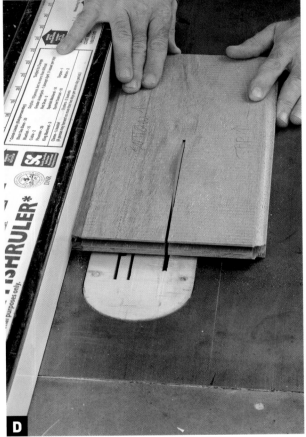

D

CUT 'EM IN TWO. Rip the rail stock to final width by separating rails on the tablesaw.

prevent exit tear-out. Now cut the cope on each end of the rail stock. **C** Wide pieces like this are usually steady enough for safe feeding, but if you feel uncomfortable with the setup or have to work with narrow stock, you can feed the workpiece with a miter gauge or a large, square piece of scrap.

3. Rip the coped rail stock into individual rails on the tablesaw. **D**

4. Assemble the door, gluing the frame joints only, or the frame and the panel if the panel is made from plywood. The assembled joint exposes the stub tenon and coped area at the ends of the door, while the inner frame reveals a handsome profile and neatly coped inside corners. **E & F**

CLEAN INSIDE AND OUT. The assembled joint reveals the cope pattern at the ends of the door, while the inner sticking forms a neat miter where the parts intersect.

Mitered Frame

A mitered frame adds an entirely different look to a door, and the miter is a valuable joint to have in your door design arsenal. The problem is that a simple miter joint isn't particularly strong by itself, and needs some form of reinforcement so that a frame will hold up over time. The simplest way to strengthen a mitered door is to add biscuits to the frame joints, and to use a plywood panel that's glued into the frame. **A**

A more traditional joinery approach that permits the use of a solid panel is making a mitered, through tenon. Although you can cut this joint by hand, the process is fussy and time-consuming. Thankfully, there's a straightforward tablesaw method that gets the job done accurately and without elaborate setups.

1. Mill through-mortises in the stiles.

2. Make a 45 degree fence from ¾-in.-thick plywood or MDF and screw it to a tablesaw sled, so that the edges of the fence are oriented 45 degrees to the saw blade. Place each stile against the fence and cut a miter at each end, aligning the cut precisely at the inside shoulder of the mortise. **B**

3. Keep your rail stock an inch or so oversized in length. Transfer the same 45 degree fence (or make another one) onto a tenoning jig and, with the rail stock clamped to the jig at a 45 degree angle, rip the cheeks of the through-tenons at each end of each rail. **C**

4. Go back to the 45 degree sled to crosscut the mitered shoulders on the rails. Square a line across the stock to indicate the final rail length, and then saw the shoulders by lowering the blade to the desired shoulder height and lining up the blade with your mark. **D**

A

EASY MITER. You can join a mitered frame with glue and biscuits—even doubling them for strength—as long as you use a plywood panel and glue it into the frame.

B

CUTOFF SLED MAKES MITERS. Screw a 45 degree fence to a tablesaw crosscut sled to cut the miters, lining up the blade with the inner shoulder of the mortise.

C

SAW THE SHOULDERS. Go back to the crosscut sled and miter the shoulders of the rails, lining up the blade with your marks.

D

ANGLE THE TENONS. Using stock that's oversized in length, use a single blade or two stacked side by side to rip the 45 degree cheeks on the rail stock.

5. Saw the tenon to width on the bandsaw, making it just shy of the length of the mortise, and then trim the miter, staying away from the shoulder line. **E** Finish the miter by paring to the line at the bench. Dry-fit the tenons and trim them so they protrude about ⅛ in. from the joint.

6. Use a slot cutter on the router table to cut the grooves in the frame, routing stopped grooves in the rails. Rout a rather shallow groove—about ¼ in. deep—to keep the tenons as strong as possible, and stop the grooves so they don't go past the ends of the tenons.

7. Bandsaw a kerf in the center of each tenon for a wedge, and make wedges to fit, using a similar approach as when wedging a drawer knob (see "Turned and Wedged Knob" on p. 61).

TRIM THE TENON. Rip the tenon to width and then saw close to the shoulder to remove the bulk of the waste.

CLAMP AND WEDGE. Assemble the door using clamps in opposing directions to pull the miters tight, and then splay each tenon inside its mortise by tapping in a wedge.

8. Dry-fit the frame and make any necessary adjustments so the joints are tight. This also gives you a practice run on arranging the clamps, which are a bit trickier to place than when assembling a standard door frame. Once everything looks good, spread glue on all the joints, assemble the panel and the frame, and tap in each wedge with a little glue. **F**

9. Once the glue has dried, plane and sand the protruding tenon flush with the frame. **G**

G

TENON KEEPS IT STRONG. The completed joint looks great from any angle, and the wedged tenon ensures the miter stays tight over time.

GLASS ADDS CLASS. Furniture maker Jan Derr used textured glass on his doors to gain visual interest as well as to cut down on visibility inside the cabinet.

Simple Glass Doors

Glass doors really dress up a cabinet and can add a practical touch if the glass is translucent, letting you see the contents behind the door. You can also use semi-transparent or textured glass if you want to light up the inside without revealing precisely what's there.

You can make a simple glass door with a single pane of glass by routing a rabbet in the back of the frame. Use a rabbeting bit equipped with a bearing

RABBET THE BACK. To rout a rabbet on the backside of the frame, use an oversized base plate and a rabbeting bit equipped with a bearing.

CHISEL IT SQUARE. Square up the rounded corners left by the bit with slicing cuts from a sharp chisel.

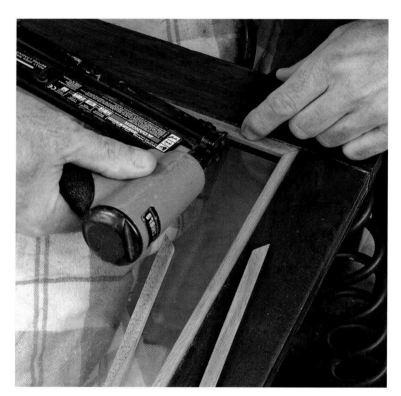

SECURE IT WITH WOOD. Round over one edge of some square stock, miter their ends, and nail through the strips and into the corner of the rabbet with a pin nailer.

that creates a ½-in.-wide rabbet, and set the depth to cut the rabbet about ⅜ in. deep, depending on the thickness of your stock. The bit will leave rounded corners, which you can square up by hand with a chisel.

Measure the rabbeted opening, and have a glass shop cut the glass about ⅛ in. smaller than your measurements. (Glass expands slightly, so you need to leave a bit of room.) There are several methods for installing the glass. The quickest and easiest is to spread a bead of silicone caulk onto the rabbet, and then lay the glass over the caulk. The back of the door isn't particularly clean-looking, though. A more traditional approach is to use glazier's points (available at framing shops), pressing them over the glass and into the rabbet, then troweling some glazing putty over the glass and points at a 45 degree angle with a putty knife. Last, you can hold the glass securely and create a neat appearance by nailing wooden strips over the glass and into the corner of the rabbets.

7 FITTING AND FINISHING DOORS

- *Fitting Doors*
- *Hinging Doors*
- *Handles and Pulls*
- *Doorstops*
- *Catches and Latches*

The big door payoff comes when you get to fit the door to its opening, hang it on the appropriate hinges, add knobs or pulls, and install a closing mechanism. This is when a cabinet comes to life and starts to look like a real piece of furniture.

If you're hanging overlay or half-overlay doors, fitting them will be a walk in the park. Simply build your doors a smidgeon oversize so you can sand and smooth any raw edges, then install them with your favorite hinges. The careful fitting of inset doors requires more concentration and time, but the look of a door nested inside its case is often worth the extra effort.

The amount of sweat involved in hinging a door and adding handles and catches is directly commensurate with the type of hardware you use. Surface-mount hinges are a breeze to install, while many types of butt hinges require careful mortising into both the case and the door, and take more time to get right. Store-bought knobs are typically quicker to install than shop-made wooden wonders. Your level of involvement should reflect the type of work you want to produce. Go the easy route if time is of the essence and you simply want to get a project done. Take the longer road if you're building an heirloom that will be passed down for generations. There's plenty of good hardware available to suit either approach or something in between.

Fitting Doors

Fitting overlay and half-overlay doors involves simple math: Build the door about ¹⁄₁₆ in. oversize, then smooth the edges with a handplane or sander after assembly. Allow about ⅛ in. of space for each rabbet in a half-overlay door, which ensures the rabbeted edges won't bind inside the case once the door is hung.

Fitting an inset door requires a more detailed approach. Just as when building inset drawers, I size my inset doors to the precise size of the case opening, which means they won't enter the case initially. This approach lets you fine-tune the fit so you can create exacting gaps, or reveals, around the door. Unless you're building a slab-type door, you won't have to worry about wood movement. Therefore, the purpose of the reveal is simply to allow the door

IT WON'T FIT. If you sized your door correctly, it shouldn't fit the case just yet. Place the door on a pair of shims, and tape it in position if necessary.

to enter the case while providing an even-looking gap all around. For most inset doors, a gap of $\frac{1}{16}$ in. or less is sufficient. You may think there's little room for error with this method, but the fitting process isn't difficult if you follow the correct steps. The key is to make adjustments using a hand plane, which lets you remove material in tiny, controllable amounts.

1. Start by placing two shims, equal in thickness to the desired reveal, onto the bottom of the case opening, then offer the door up to the case. If the door won't fit into the opening at all, remove some material off one of the stiles, either by making a rip cut on the tablesaw or with a few swipes from a hand plane. At this point, the top of the door shouldn't enter the case. **A**

2. With the door sitting on the shims, check the gap along the hinge stile. Chances are the gap is tapered, which means either the door or the case isn't perfectly square. Note the amount of taper and, at the bench, use a plane to remove the same amount of taper, but from the appropriate area on the bottom of the door—not its side. **B** Keep test-fitting the door as you plane.

3. When the hinge side and bottom gaps are consistent, trim the top of the door to create a gap of about $\frac{1}{32}$ in. If the top and bottom edges of the opening are parallel, you can trim the door on the tablesaw, registering its bottom edge against the rip fence. **C** Otherwise, use a handplane to cut the

work SMART

Small squares of plastic laminate, cut on the tablesaw or chopsaw, make great shims for fitting doors. Countertop laminate, which is slightly less than $\frac{1}{16}$ in. thick, is perfect for most door reveals.

PLANE THE BOTTOM. Hand-plane the bottom of the door until it is parallel to the bottom of the opening while the hinge stile is pressed against the side of the opening.

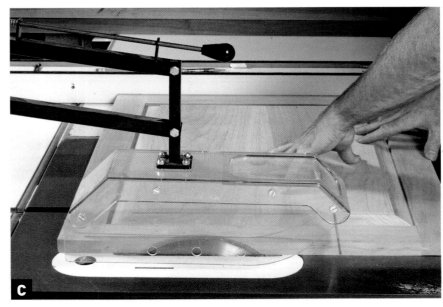

CUT DOWN THE HEIGHT. Place the bottom edge of the door against the rip fence and trim about $\frac{1}{32}$ in. from the top.

CHECK AGAIN. Inspect the gap at the top of the door while holding the hinge stile tight against the case.

appropriate taper. Make sure the gap is consistent along its length and equal to the gap at the bottom while holding the hinge stile tight against the opening. **D**

4. At this point, the gaps on the sides of the door should need to be widened to allow for hinging. However, if you've started with too narrow a door and the gap is 1/16 in. or more, skip this step and go to the next.

To create clearance for the hinges, begin by ripping enough from the hinge stile to create a combined side gap of about 1/16 in. You can do this on the tablesaw or with a handplane, taking relatively aggressive cuts. **E**

CLEARANCE FOR HINGES. Take aggressive cuts with a plane to remove about 1/16 in. of wood on the hinge stile.

5. After installing the hinges (see "Hinging Doors" on p. 141), check the reveal along the non-hinged stile. Typically, the gap will still be too small at this point, and may exhibit a small amount of taper. **F** To provide clearance, remove the door from the case and plane a slight back-bevel onto the non-hinged stile, at the same time removing any taper and producing a consistent gap. **G**

6. Once again, hang the door on its hinges and check the reveals. The fitted door should have a consistent gap of ⅟₁₆ in. or less all the way around the cabinet opening. **H**

STILL TOO TIGHT. With the door hinged to the case, check the opposite edge, noting the amount of gap and taper.

PLANE A BACK-BEVEL. A hand-planed back-bevel of just a degree or two allows a door to close easily without its inner edge smacking the edge of the opening.

GOOD ALL AROUND. A well-fitted door should have consistent, even reveals on all four sides.

PRE-HINGING FACE FRAMES

If your cabinet includes face frames, you may choose to fit the doors to the frames before attaching the frames to the case. This simplifies door installation because the fitting and hinging can be comfortably done with the parts flat on a bench. However, be aware that your success depends upon stout frames made with mortise-and-tenon joinery or other strong connections that are able to resist racking.

DOORS BEFORE CASE. On cabinets with face frames, it's possible to fit and hinge the doors before attaching the frame to the case, letting you work more comfortably on a flat surface.

DETERMINING HINGE SETBACK

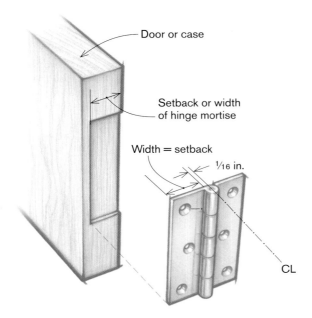

Proper hinge setback minimizes barrel protrusion while preventing a door from binding when opened.

Door or case

Setback or width of hinge mortise

Width = setback

$\frac{1}{16}$ in.

CL

To determine proper setback, measure from the long edge of a hinge leaf to the center of the hinge pin, then subtract $\frac{1}{16}$ in.

Hinging Doors

Once you've fit a door to its opening, the next step is to lay out the hinges on the case and door. Generally, you can locate paired hinges so they're a few inches from the top and bottom of the door, perhaps in line with the inner edge of the rails for a visually unifying effect. If the door is particularly tall or heavy, adding a third hinge between the pair is a good idea. It can be located in the center of the door or offset a few inches upward to resist the extra force at the top of the door.

You also need to determine the setback distance for a hinge. Setback is the amount that a hinge leaf extends into the case or door. Once you've determined the setback, you're ready to cut the mortise for the leaves.

Typically, each leaf is mortised into both case and door, with the mortise depth equal to the thickness of the leaves, though it will depend on the specific type of hinge you're using. Certain hinges, such as those with extra-thin leaves or large-diameter knuckles, will need their mortises cut a bit deeper, or the reveal will be too large. If you're in doubt, inspect the hinge. Hold it in the closed position with its leaves parallel to each other. If the gap between the leaves is too big, you'll need to make the mortises deeper. Then test your mortise depth on a couple pieces of scrap that you temporarily connect to the hinge to assess the gap.

It can be awkward to rout or chisel mortises in an assembled case, so it's often wise to cut your mortises in the case before gluing it up. After assembling the case and fitting the door, you can transfer the mating mortise locations to the door.

LAY THEM ON TOP. Surface-mount hinges, like these butter-fly hinges, are the easiest to install because you simply lay them on the case and door, and then install the screws.

Surface-mount hinges

By far the easiest type of hinge to install, a surface-mount hinge lays over the face of both case and door, and simply needs to be aligned over both parts with the appropriate reveal between them.

1. Fit the door, then place it on or in the case (depending on the style of door) and position the hinges, centering the barrel over the reveal.

2. Screw the leaves to the door first, using only one of the screw holes in each leaf. Be sure to drill pilot holes, and lube the screws with a bit of bees-wax or paraffin before screwing them home. Then

work
SMART

With standard butt hinges, the fitting process involves quite a bit of back-and-forth, hanging the door and then removing it a number of times. If you have a lot of doors to hang, it's worth considering loose-pin hinges, which allow you to remove the pin from the hinge barrel, easily separating the leaves without having to remove any screws.

attach the case leaves, placing the appropriate shims between the door and the case, and again using only one screw per leaf.

3. Check the fit of the door. If you need to make small adjustments, back off either the case screws or the door screws, adjust the door, and install the remaining screws. Then retighten the first set of screws. **A**

Standard butt hinges

Traditional butt hinges require mortising into either the door and case, or just the door, depending on the thickness of their leaves. An alternative to this style of hinge is the no-mortise hinge, which has thin leaves that either nest within each other or rest side by side when the door is closed, allowing you to surface-mount the hinge to the inside of the case and door. The following installation method works for both the case mortise and the door mortise.

NO FUSSY MORTISE. The leaves on these no-mortise hinges fold together side by side, allowing you to screw them sim-ply to the surface of the door and case without creating an unsightly gap.

DOOR-HOLDING JIG

These simple wood and steel hangers are made using thin tie-plates (available at lumberyards) that are designed to connect house framing members together. The hangars let you fit and hang a door with the work lying horizontal on your bench, which simplifies the process. You'll need a pair for each door, so it's smart to make at least four for tackling paired doors when necessary. Screws driven into countersunk holes hold the parts together. The only critical measurement is to locate the door support so it holds a specific door thickness flush with the case.

HANDS-FREE HELP. These shop-made hangers support the door in a horizontal position, allowing you to fit and hinge a door with the work flat on the bench.

DOOR HANGER

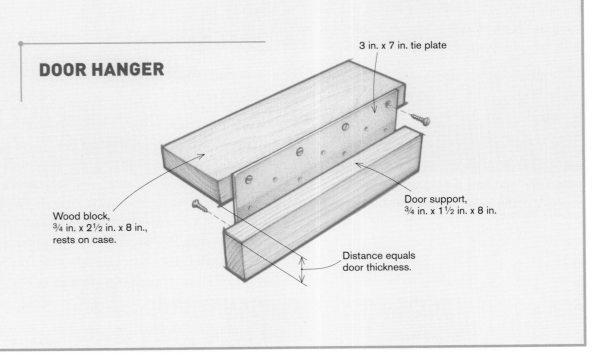

3 in. x 7 in. tie plate

Wood block,
¾ in. x 2½ in. x 8 in.,
rests on case.

Door support,
¾ in. x 1½ in. x 8 in.

Distance equals
door thickness.

KNIFE THE OUTLINE. Use a sharp knife to scribe the hinge outline into the work.

NO-FUSS DEPTH. Set the correct hinge mortise depth by holding a leaf up to the bit and adjusting the router until the tip of the cutter is level with the leaf.

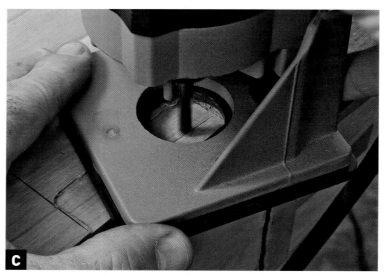

TRIM INSIDE THE LINES. Feeding the router freehand, cut just inside the scribe lines. One hand low on the base steadies the router as you cut.

1. Position the hinge for the correct setback, then hold it firmly and use a sharp knife to incise its outlines into the case or door. **A**

2. Chuck a small straight bit into a small router (a trim router is ideal), and set the cutting depth equal to the thickness of one leaf, or a bit more if your leaves are extra-thin. **B**

3. Holding the router freehand, rout as close to your scribed lines as you dare. You should be able to get within 1/16 in. or less of the lines, since you're removing very little wood and there won't be much pull on the router. To create a uniform mortise depth, keep the router steady without tipping it. **C** Chisel to the shoulder lines by hand, first chopping the ends of the mortise, and then carefully paring the back edge. Take small cuts up to the line, then make a final cut with the tip of the chisel directly in your scribed line. **D**

5. Drill pilot holes for one of the screws in each leaf on both the case and door. Install the hinge in the door, then install the hinged door to the case.

D

CUT ON THE LINE. Define the shoulders of the mortise by chiseling the ends first and then the back shoulder. Carefully pare close to the line, and then make a final chopping cut right on the line.

E

TIGHT AND FLUSH. A well-fitted, high-quality extruded hinge sits level with the surface of the door and case, and fits snugly at the shoulders of the mortises.

Check the fit. If you need to make adjustments, use the same procedure as when installing a surface-mount hinge, driving only one set of screws before committing all of them. Once you're happy with the fit, install the remaining screws. **E**

Cup hinges

Also known as Euro hinges, cup hinges are big pieces of relatively unattractive gear. However, they're only visible inside the case, so they are often used even in high-end projects. Still, I prefer other less obtrusive hinges, such as butt hinges or knife hinges for my best work. Cup hinges are a sensible choice for kitchen cabinets, where you have many doors to hang, and where no one is going to be too fussy about the interiors. The big advantages to cup hinges is that they are easy to install and can be simply and precisely adjusted afterward. There are many styles to choose from, including overlay, half-overlay, and inset. You can buy cup hinges that attach directly to a face frame or inside the case.

You'll need a 35mm cup-hinge bit (a 1⅜ in. Forstner bit will work in a pinch) and a drill press to drill the hinge holes in the door. Alternatively, there are commercial jigs that work with 35mm bits chucked into a handheld drill.

HOLES FOR HINGES. Use the drill press to bore the hinge holes to the proper depth. Work against a fence that has a rabbet at the bottom to provide chip clearance.

1. Clamp a fence to the drill press table to align the edge of the door relative to the bit. (Check the manufacturer's instructions for the correct setback.) Set the depth stop for the correct depth, which is typically ½ in. Mark centerlines on the door stile, then hold the door firmly by hand and drill on your mark. **A**

2. At the bench, use a square to align the hinge to the edge of the door, and drill pilot holes for the screws using a self-centering bit. **B** Drive the screws through the hinge to secure it to the door.

3. Hang the door by holding it in place and marking where the hinge's baseplate contacts the case. Remove the baseplate from the hinge, and install it with screws to the case. If you're using case-mounted hinges on a case with a face frame, simply nail and glue support blocks to the case side to bring the baseplate flush to the case opening. **C**

4. Once the door is hung, you can adjust the hinge precisely to fit the door to the case. In a matter of moments a door can be adjusted three ways: forward and rearward, side to side, and up and down. A Phillips-style screwdriver will work for this,

SQUARE AND CENTER. Align the hinge square to the edge of the door, then use a self-centering bit to drill pilot holes through the hinge and into the back of the door.

BLOCK IT FLUSH. When a face frame extends past a case side or divider, add blocks of wood to the case to bring the hinge's base plate flush to the frame.

A

RABBET IT RIGHT. Close the hinge with the leaves parallel, and check that your rabbet depth equals the thickness of one leaf plus the diameter of the barrel's pin.

C

but it's best to use a specialty screwdriver made expressly for the screws that come with the hinge (one brand is called Posi-drive), which ensures a positive grip and avoids stripping the screws.

Continuous hinges

Often referred to as a piano hinge, a continuous hinge is one of the strongest you can use. In effect a long butt hinge with an uninterrupted pin and numerous mounting screws, it works very well for large or extra-heavy doors. Small continuous hinges can be surface-mounted to the case and door. Larger hinges, with leaves ⅝ in. or wider, require

setting into the door to avoid a large, unsightly reveal between the case and door.

1. Instead of mortising, you cut a rabbet the full length of the door and install the hinge to fit. To determine the correct rabbet depth, close the hinge so that the leaves parallel, then measure the thickness of one leaf plus the diameter of the barrel's pin. Mill the rabbet to that depth. **A** I typically cut the rabbet on the tablesaw using a dado blade, but you could use a router equipped with a straight bit and an edge guide instead.

work
SMART

Continuous hinges can easily be cut to custom lengths with a hacksaw. Close the hinge, clamp it in a vise, and mark the cutline so it falls on one of the joint lines on the barrel. Smooth any rough edges with a fine file.

ONE-SIDED MORTISE. Install one leaf into the rabbet in the door edge, then surface-mount the opposite leaf to the case.

2. Drill pilot holes for the screws and mount the hinge to the door by securing one leaf into the rabbet. Hang the door by surface-mounting the opposite leaf onto the case. **B**

Barrel hinges

Barrel hinges, which are mortised into the edge of the door and case, are a good choice when you don't want to see any hardware, inside or outside the case. They're also great for bi-fold doors, which are hinged together in pairs (see p. 106). One variety, commonly called a Soss hinge, requires making multiple stepped mortises for installation, and offers little if any adjustment should your door need some tweaking after installation. A straight barrel hinge is much easier to install, though layout must be precise since, like a Soss hinge, very little adjustment is allowed. The following installation procedure

STRONG BUT FUSSY. This Soss hinge will support heavy doors and is quite elegant to look at, but installation requires making multi-step mortises.

SIDE BY SIDE. After clamping two doors together with their ends flush, and striking a line square across both edges, use a spade bit to drill a hole for the hinge, stopping when the tape sweeps the shavings from the surface.

applies to paired doors, but the basic approach can also be used to install a single door.

1. Clamp a pair of doors together with their ends flush, and lay out the hinge location by striking a line square across the edge of the doors. For these particular barrel hinges, known as Italian hinges, I use a ⁷⁄₁₆-in. spade bit whose edges I had ground and filed in order to reduce the hole diameter for a better fit. Use a piece of tape wrapped around the bit to flag the correct depth, and drill as squarely as possible into the edge of the door. **A**

2. Install the hinge into both door edges, tapping each barrel in flush to the surface and then tightening the hinge screw to expand the hinge in the hole. **B**

Knife hinges

Considered by many to be the Rolls-Royce of door hinges, knife hinges add a unique touch of elegance to any box or cabinet, providing silky-smooth action and emanating a jewelry-like presence. There are two styles: straight hinges for overlay doors, and offset hinges for inset doors. I prefer two-part hinges because the leaves, or blades, separate, making for easier installation.

work
SMART

When choosing offset knife hinges, be sure to specify right-hand hinges for doors that are hinged on the right side of the case, and left-hand hinges for left-swinging doors.

B

EXPAND IT TO FIT. Install the hinge so each barrel is level with the surface of the door, and then tighten them in their holes by turning a screw in each barrel.

TWO STYLES OF KNIFE HINGES

Straight

Use for overlay doors

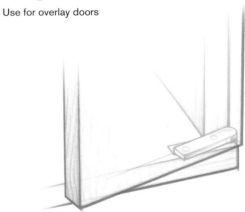

Offset

Use for inset doors

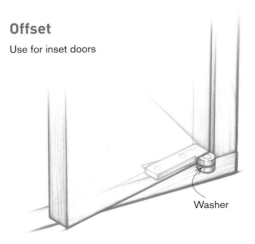

Washer

Hinging Doors ■ 149

POSITION IT WITH A BIT. Pull the knife hinge blade inward against a drill bit that's half the diameter of the blade pin hole. Then scribe around the blade with a sharp knife.

SMOOTH AND SHINY. A nicely fitted knife hinge sits flush in its mortises in the door and case, and looks like custom jewelry from the outside.

1. Cut the hinge mortises in the case before assembly. You can use the same layout and routing procedure as when installing a butt hinge, as described previously in this chapter.

2. When fitting the door, the key is to create top and bottom reveals that equal the thickness of the hinge washer. If you get slightly out of whack and trim the door a tad too small, you can shim under the blades with slips of veneer or sheets of paper cut to fit. To lay out a straight hinge on a door, begin by selecting a drill bit that's slightly larger than one-half of the pin's diameter, and tape it to the edge of the door. Slip the hinge blade onto the bit, pulling it toward the center of the door, then scribe around the hinge with a knife. **A** Cut the mortise as you did the case mortise.

3. Screw the pin blades into their case mortise, press each mating blade onto its pin, then slide the door between the blades. As with butt hinges, begin by installing a single screw for each hinge, then check the fit of the door. Make any adjustments by lengthening one or both of the door mortises with a chisel, then drive the final screws. **B**

Handles and Pulls

The finishing touch on any door is its pull. You can choose from a plethora of commercially available handles and pulls in a variety of styles and materials including metal, wood, and even stone. Alternatively, many woodworkers prefer to make their own pulls, which is a great way to personalize your work.

Like the turned drawer pull in Chapter 3 (see p. 61), you can use the same approach for door pulls, turning them to include a tenon that extends through the stock and is wedged from behind. Or you can carve pulls in any shape you wish, then cut a round-ended tenon and let it protrude through the door at the back, wedging it like you would a turned tenon.

BUY YOUR HANDLE. Commercial door pulls come in a variety of styles, shapes, and materials, including colored metal (left), wood in many species, and natural stone (right).

NICE TO TOUCH. These shop-made carved pulls flare outward slightly, inviting the hand.

SOFT AND SECURE. Wedged from behind for strength, the pull's through-tenon sits a bit proud of the surface and is gently rounded over for a pillowed effect.

A

ROUGH BUT REFINED. These paired pulls were sawn side by side from a single piece of maple burl, allowing their natural contours to complement each other.

ANGLE ONE END. At the top of the mortise, chisel an inward slope to accommodate the swing of the pull that fits inside.

A

Burl pulls

One of the simplest methods for attaching pulls is to screw them on from behind. To jazz up the front of a door, consider using burled wood, which displays outrageous figure that's perfect for such small things as pulls.

1. Using a bandsaw or tablesaw, slice the burl to a comfortable thickness of about ½ in. Cut a gentle miter at each end, and then sand the sawn surfaces smooth.

2. Drill screw clearance holes through the door, countersinking them on the back side. Then spread glue on the back of the pulls, and screw them to the door from behind.

3. A pair of burl handles work well together, especially if they're sawn in sequence from the same burl. **A** Be sure to sand down any sharp points or other protrusions common to burled wood so the handles are comfortable to the touch.

Sliding door pulls

When you have one door that slides behind another, you need a way to grasp the edge of the concealed door. This pivoting pull provides the perfect solution.

1. Before assembling the door, cut a square-ended mortise into the edge of the appropriate door stile. Then chisel a slight, undercut angle at the top end of the mortise using a mortising chisel. **A** An angle of about 10 degrees is sufficient.

2. Mill the pull stock so it slips easily into the mortise, and shape it to fit on the bandsaw. **B** Be sure to cut a long miter at the back of the pull so it clears the rear of the mortise when pivoting during use.

3. Slip the pull into the mortise and drill through both the pull and door stile to accept a ⅛-in.-dia. pin. **C**

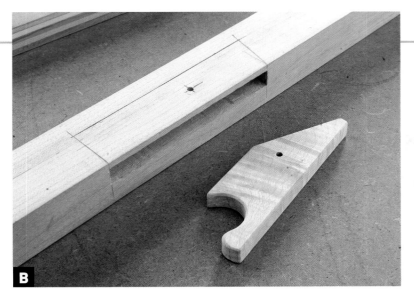

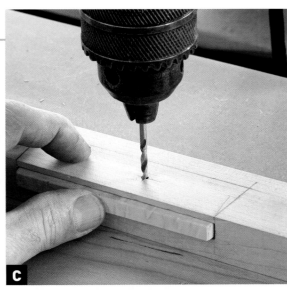

SHAPED FOR ACTION. Mill a piece of wood to the length of the mortise and slightly wider than its depth, then shape it on the bandsaw with a long miter at the back of the top and a hooked area on the bottom.

DRILL FOR A PIN. Slip the finished pull into the mortise with its outside edge parallel with the stile, and drill through both for a ⅛-in.-dia. pin.

DRILL FOR A PLUG. Use a Forstner bit to drill a shallow hole in the face of the pull, supporting the angled end of the pull with an angled scrap.

SHAPED LIKE A BUTTON. Glue in a long-grain plug (the author used cherry to contrast with the maple pull), and carve it to a button shape with a chisel.

4. Drill into the face of the pull near its top edge to accept a wood plug. Support the pull with a scrap piece cut to a complementary angle. **D** Glue a plug into the hole using a contrasting wood, and carve it into a domed-shape button using a bench chisel. **E**

work SMART

The strongest material to use for small pins is bamboo, which has great tensile strength. Luckily, bamboo is readily available at your local supermarket where it's sold as skewers for grilling, typically in diameters of ⅛ in.

PUSH, THEN PULL.
Pushing on the dowel button extends the lower part of the pull for finger access.

F

G

5. Install the pull into the mortise, glue the pin in place, then install the door. When the door is slid behind another, the contrasting button provides a clue as to where to place a finger. **F** Push on the button, and the pull pivots outward for finger access. **G**

work SMART

To prevent a door from banging against the case or clattering in use, you can apply the same cushioned bumpers that soften the closing of drawers, as shown on p. 66.

Doorstops

All doors need some kind of a closing stop to prevent them from swinging inward beyond the plane of the case, and stressing the hinges. Sometimes a simple approach is all that's needed to stop a door. Polish up a small strip of good-looking wood and nail it to the case behind the door, perhaps at the top and the bottom. Voila! Instant doorstop.

With overlay or half-overlay doors, the case itself serves as the stop. With inset doors on cabinets with face frames, you can inset the top and bottom case pieces so their front edges are partially exposed within the frame opening to act as doorstops. Be sure to conceal any raw plywood edges with edge-banding before assembling the case (see the drawing on the facing page). However, when that's not feasible due to your cabinet design, there are other options for stopping doors.

BUILT-IN DOOR STOPS

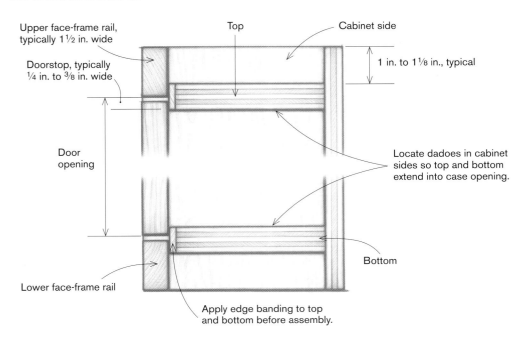

Upper face-frame rail, typically 1½ in. wide

Doorstop, typically ¼ in. to ⅜ in. wide

Door opening

Lower face-frame rail

Top

Cabinet side

1 in. to 1⅛ in., typical

Locate dadoes in cabinet sides so top and bottom extend into case opening.

Bottom

Apply edge banding to top and bottom before assembly.

Magnet doorstops

You can make a great doorstop using rare earth magnets, which keep a door closed in the right position by magnetic attraction. Commonly available from many woodworking mail order catalogs, rare earth magnets come in various diameters. Generally, a pair of ⅜-in.-dia. magnets is sufficient to pull a standard cabinet door closed. Mortise one of the magnets into a shallow hole in the case, and another in the top edge of the door, with a Forstner bit, making sure the two holes are aligned with each other. Epoxy the magnets into the holes, orienting their polarity for attraction. Otherwise, your door will never close.

MAGNETIC ATTRACTION. Gluing a magnet into the edge of the door, with a corresponding magnet in the case, offers plenty of pull to keep a door secure.

SOFT ACTION. Blum's Blumotion soft-closing mechanism consists of a piston inside a plastic sleeve that's housed in a metal enclosure.

Soft-closing stops

If you're using self-closing hinges, there's a nifty piece of hardware that's worth investigating. This "soft-closing mechanism" is a piston-like cylinder that slowly retracts as the spring action of the hinges presses the door against it, causing the door to close softly and silently.

One type, which is available on cup hinges only, is incorporated into the hinge itself. Another variety is a separate piece of hardware that you install near the non-hinged side of the door, as I'll discuss here.

DOUBLE DOOR DEVICE. For paired doors, install two closers onto a single block of wood, aligning the front of each device with the front of the block.

READY TO CLOSE. Glue and nail the block to the underside of the case, centered over the doors and flush with the back of the case rail.

1. The closing mechanism comes in three parts, and should be assembled before installation. The plastic piston fits into a plastic sleeve, which in turn fits into a metal housing. **A**

2. For double-door cabinets with overhanging face frames, screw two closers side by side onto a spacer block whose thickness equals the frame overhang. **B**

3. Glue and screw the block to the underside of the case top, so that the face of the metal housing is flush with the back of the door. **C** When the doors are closed, the plastic pistons retract slowly until the door rests flush with the case.

Wooden flipper stops

One of the slickest types of shop-made stops is the flipper catch made famous by furniture maker James Krenov and his teaching staff at the College of the Redwoods in Fort Bragg, Calif. This particular catch, designed for paired, rabbeted doors that nest together, features spring-loaded "flipper" catches that sit in shallow mortises cut in the underside of the case top, and exert gentle pressure on the top of each door to keep it closed. One of the two wooden catches incorporates a carved node that serves as a backstop for the captured door, which is closed first.

The same approach works for a single door if you follow the procedure for making a flipper with a node for a captured door, as described on p. 158.

PRESS THE DOORS CLOSED.
A pair of flipper stops creates friction against the tops of a nesting pair of doors when they're closed. The protruding node on the left-hand flipper serves as a backstop for the captured door.

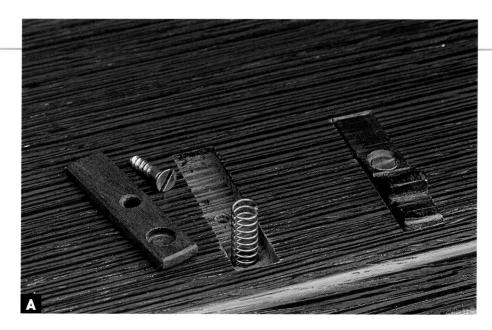

RAMPED AT THE BOTTOM. Inset a pillow-shaped slip of wood into a shallow case mortise beneath the doors to maintain door lift and a consistent reveal.

1. For the first-opening door, shape a rectangular flipper to include a pillow-like raised pad at its forward end. Cut a shallow mortise in the underside of the case top to accept the flipper, making the mortise slightly deeper than the thickness of the flipper body. Drill and countersink a screw hole in the center of the flipper's exposed face. Drill a flat-bottomed hole into the forward section of the inner face and a corresponding hole in the case mortise to accept a small spring. **A**

2. For the captured door, make a similar flipper and mortise in the same fashion, but this time shape the flipper to include a raised node that will stop the door flush with the case.

3. Install the flippers into their mortises, and drive in the screws just to the point where each flipper presses firmly against the top of the door when it's closed.

4. To complete the stop system, inlay a small strip of wood into the case bottom, straddling the underside of both doors. The strip, which should be proud of the case by the desired amount of reveal, acts as a pressure bar to keep the doors pressed firmly against the flippers above while maintaining an even reveal at the bottom. **B**

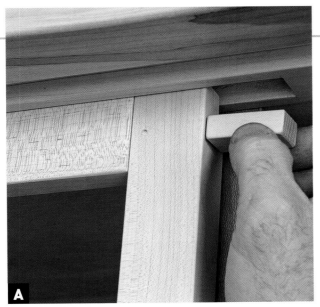

A

work**SMART**

When making a stopped groove as part of a three-door configuration, I typically mill the groove in the left-hand section of the track, which favors the majority of us right-handers in the world. (No slight intended to my lefty friends.)

STOP AT THE TOP. Cut the door groove an inch or so longer than necessary, position the door, then fill the excess space with a wood stop block.

Sliding doorstops

For pairs of doors that slide on wooden tracks, the case sides serve as stops. But for three or more doors, you'll need to stop at least one of the extra doors in the middle, which can be done by simply milling a stopped groove in the track. However, it can be difficult to calculate the precise length of the stopped groove before installing the track. Instead, it's easier and more accurate to mill the groove an inch or two longer than needed, and then, after attaching the track to the case, install a wooden filler block at the end of the groove to halt the door exactly where you want.

1. To calculate the size of the stop for the upper track, place the door in its grooves and position it precisely where it needs to stop. Then measure the excess space in the track groove and cut a block of wood to fit. **A**

2. Fit a stop block for the bottom track in the same manner. You can trim each block so it sits flush with the top of the track, or size it so it sits about ⅛ in. proud to accentuate it. **B** For durability, orient both blocks so the door bumps against end-grain, not face-grain. A couple of pins or brads are all that's necessary to hold the blocks in the tracks.

B

SHOW 'EM OFF. Size sliding doorstops so they sit slightly proud of the track for visual effect.

CAUGHT BY A BALL. This bullet catch, which consists of a spring-loaded tip captured in a metal sleeve, is pressed into a hole drilled at the top of the door. A metal strike inside the case engages the ball when the door is closed.

Catches and Latches

To keep a door closed, install self-closing hinges, which are available in many styles and which employ springs that push the door closed. Doors with free-swinging hinges, on the other hand, need a catch mechanism.

Spring-loaded catches

A bullet catch is one of the simplest types of door catches. It consists of two parts: a bullet-shaped, spring-loaded tip that projects from a small cylinder mounted in the edge of a door, and a striker plate that's mounted on the case. Most doors fare well with a single catch, though you can install one in the top and one in the bottom edge of a door for extra purchase. Installing a bullet catch is a simple matter of drilling a hole in the edge of the door,

CATCH 'N' LATCH. Ball-and-latch catches will keep a pair of heavy doors closed. The ball housing screwed to the underside of the case accepts a mating tongue plate that's screwed to the back of the door.

SLIDE IT TO LOCK. This sliding bolt catch is mortised into the back of the door stile, and engages a small hole drilled into the case.

pressing the cylinder part into the hole, and then tacking the metal strike to the case.

Somewhat similar in style is the ball-and-latch catch, a two-piece mechanism consisting of a tongue plate that attaches to the back of the door, and a mating housing that attaches to the case. The housing contains a pair of spring-loaded balls that pinch the tongue in place to hold the door closed. This mechanism provides much stronger closure than a bullet catch, and the spring tension against the balls can be adjusted somewhat. The downsides are that the tongue can be fussy to locate properly, and the latching action is noisier than other catches. However, ball-and-latch catches are a good choice for doors that need strong closure, such as heavy doors or doors subject to stress, such as those found on boats or other moving objects.

Sliding and spinning latches

For overlapping paired doors, you typically need to employ a latch mechanism to secure the trapped door. There are several styles of latches for this purpose. One of the most elegant solutions is the sliding bolt latch, which is mortised into the back of the door. You drill a corresponding hole in the case to receive the bolt. To latch the first-opening door, a half-mortise lock is appropriate, especially for period pieces. Installation is the same as when using mortise locks on drawers (see p. 68).

A more rustic approach to securing both doors involves installing a sliding bolt or latch on one door, and then screwing a pivoting shop-made latch to the face of the same door. To secure the second door, simply rotate the latch so it straddles both doors. Down and dirty perhaps, but it gets the job done in a humble and straightforward manner.

LOCKED TO ANOTHER. Half-mortise locks work very well on paired rabbeted doors to keep the first-opening door secured to the captured door.

TURN IT TO OPEN. A hand-carved latch is attached with a single screw that allows it to pivot vertically to open a door.

8 SPECIAL DOORS AND DETAILS

- *Pocket Doors*

- *Sliding Doors*

- *Traditional Divided-Light Door*

- *Shoji-Style Divided-Light Door*

- *Arched-Top Door*

- *Curved Frame- and-Panel Doors*

- *Curved Glass-Faceted Door*

- *Beads, Inlay, and Other Decorative Effects*

Beyond the basic door is a world of exciting possibilities, filled with special-purpose doors that slide or retract into the case, doors with multiple panes of glass, curved doors in many shapes and sizes, and doors augmented with inlays and other decorative effects. Truth is, there are far too many types of specialized doors for one book to cover. That being said, in this chapter I'll discuss several kinds that many woodworkers will find useful and appealing.

The doors on the following pages are unique. Some address specific circumstances, such as when doors need to retract into the case or slide by each other instead of swinging on hinges. Some are just plain fun, like a "split panel" made from live-edged boards glued edge to edge, or curved or arched doors that depart from the rectilinear world of flat and straight. Others follow traditional design precepts that woodworkers have used for centuries, such as divided-light doors that hold individual panes of glass.

Whatever your needs or design passions, I encourage you to try your hand at the door ideas presented here. Incorporating these ideas into your woodworking repertoire will help you move your furniture beyond the ordinary and into the realm of the truly special.

SPLIT PANEL. Woodworker Jan Derr made an unusual panel by edge-gluing two natural-edged boards together to create a gap in the middle.

Pocket Doors

Sometimes referred to as "flipper doors," pocket doors can be opened and then slid back into the case to present a clear view of the cabinet's contents without the doors extended. It's a great system to use for entertainment centers or other projects where you want a traditional look with the doors closed to hide the equipment, but need an unobstructed view when they're open.

HOW A POCKET DOOR WORKS

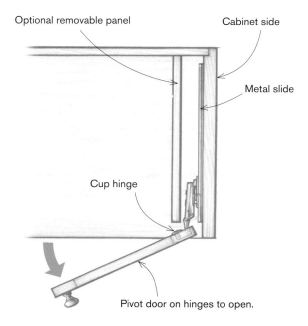

Optional removable panel

Cabinet side

Metal slide

Cup hinge

Pivot door on hinges to open.

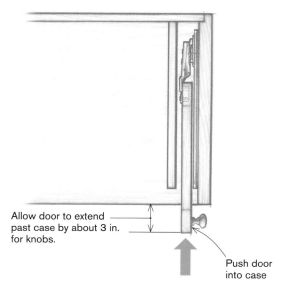

Allow door to extend past case by about 3 in. for knobs.

Push door into case

work SMART

To conceal your doors when they're in the case, you can create a "pocket" for each door to retract into. Building a pocket is optional; the doors will work fine without them, but it helps to tidy up the interior. Simply install a vertical panel, setting it back about 1 in. from the inside face of the door. Attach it with screws to the top and bottom of the case so it's removable during the construction phase, which helps with locating the slide hardware.

JUST LIKE DRAWER SLIDES. Pocket doors mount to a cabinet via cup hinges attached to the door, which in turn are secured to ball-bearing slides screwed to the case. Adjust the door to fit once you've connected the hardware.

PULL AND PUSH. Open the doors as you normally would, then simply push them back into the case to conceal them.

Pocket door hardware incorporates cup hinges that connect the doors to drawer-type metal slides on the case. The system will also work for lift-up or flipper doors that open upward, such as in a stereo cabinet. Before designing a cabinet with pocket doors, be sure to buy the appropriate hardware first, and make sure it suits the type of doors you'll be using, whether overlay, half-overlay, or inset. Also, size the case and door to allow enough depth in the case for the door to retract while allowing its edge to project from the case a few inches to access knobs and handles.

1. Make and fit the door or doors, and attach the hinges just as you would ordinary cup hinges (see p. 145).

2. Install the slide mechanism in the case by referring to the manufacturer's directions. The process is similar to installing metal drawer slides (see p. 143).

3. Attach the doors to the slide mechanism in the case. Adjust the door for a precise fit by loosening or tightening the screws on the hinge baseplate. **A**

4. On these overlay doors, simply pull them open as usual, and then push them back into the case. **B & C**

Sliding Doors

A wooden door sliding on a wooden track moves with an indescribably satisfying action. Fortunately, sliding doors and the wooden tracks that guide them are relatively easy to make. If you're making a pair of doors that slide by each other on parallel tracks, it's usually best to size the doors equally and dimension the case so that the innermost stiles overlap when the doors are closed.

With three or more sliding doors, which still require two adjacent tracks, you can also size the case opening so that adjacent door stiles overlap with the doors closed. However, this may cause an open door to project into an adjacent case opening, possibly impeding access. I prefer to design my case opening width to match the total combined width of all the doors so they meet edge to edge with only a hairline gap between them when closed. This keeps the edges of the doors flush with or slightly inset from the center case dividers when the doors are opened. Whatever your approach, it's wise to make a full-scale drawing of the setup before committing to the case or door sizes. That way, you can ensure the desired door locations, whether open or closed.

SLIDING DOOR ANATOMY

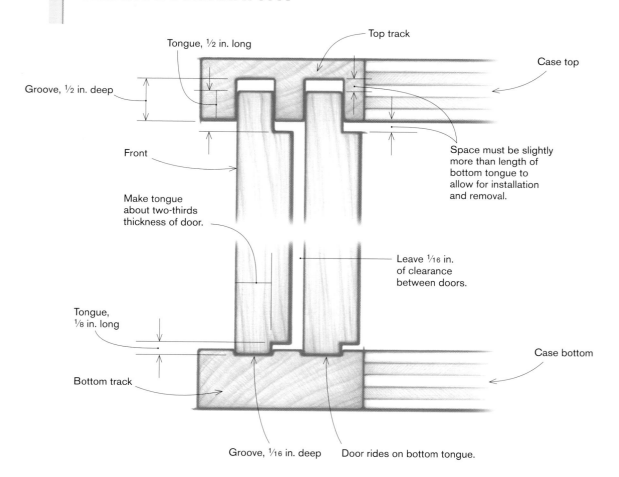

Tongue, 1/2 in. long

Top track

Case top

Groove, 1/2 in. deep

Front

Space must be slightly more than length of bottom tongue to allow for installation and removal.

Make tongue about two-thirds thickness of door.

Leave 1/16 in. of clearance between doors.

Tongue, 1/8 in. long

Case bottom

Bottom track

Groove, 1/16 in. deep   Door rides on bottom tongue.

A

GARBAGE GOES HERE. On the lower tracks, chisel a ramped recess at the end of each groove to capture dust and debris that might otherwise build up there.

Build the case first, then make the top and bottom track. Keep in mind that the groove in the top track must be deep enough to allow the door to lift out of its bottom track in order to remove (and install) the door. The bottom grooves should be kept shallow to help prevent dirt and debris from accumulating. A depth of $\frac{1}{16}$ in. to $\frac{1}{8}$ in. is plenty to guide the door. Once you've fitted and glued the track to the case, make the doors to fit, rabbeting their top and bottom edges to create tongues that glide smoothly in the track without rattling. Remember to make the rails wide enough to slip into the upper and lower tracks.

1. Use a dado blade on the tablesaw to plow stopped grooves in the top and bottom track, and chisel the end of each groove square to act as a door stop. On the lower track, I chisel a small ramped recess at the end of each groove to serve as a "dust bin" that helps prevent dirt and debris from building up in the corners. **A**

B

CUT THE TONGUES. To create tongues that fit the track grooves, rabbet the top and bottom edges of the door.

2. Size the doors to fit the grooves in the track, using a dado blade on the tablesaw to cut a rabbet in the top and bottom edges to create tongues that slide easily in the grooves. If the door is particularly tall, clamp a featherboard to the table to steady the work, ensuring a tongue of consistent width. **B** Make the tongue a bit fat, then refine its width with a few swipes from a shoulder plane for a precise sliding fit into the groove.

C

READY TO SLIDE. Smooth and wax the tracks and the tongues on the bottom of the doors for silky-smooth action.

D

UP, THEN DOWN. Install the door by slipping its top edge into the upper track, then lowering it onto the bottom track.

3. Plane the underside of the bottom tongue straight and smooth, and then sand it and all of the tongue and track surfaces as smooth as you can. Apply a couple of coats of a light penetrating finish like 1-lb.-cut shellac to the tongues and the tracks, then wax the finish. In operation, the door should ride on the tongue, not the rabbeted edge. **C**

4. Fit each door into its respective track by first slipping the top tongue into its groove, and then lowering the door into the bottom track. **D** Check the slide action; the door should glide in its track with an easy sideways push. If necessary, smooth any high spots with a sanding block and fine paper.

Traditional Divided-Light Door

A divided-light door includes a wooden framework that consists of horizontal muntins and vertical mullions joined in a grid work that's secured to the door frame. Each section of the grid houses a separate pane of glass, called a *light*. A door can include any number of lights, though four, six, eight, or nine is common, depending on the door's size.

There are several router bit sets available for making divided-light cope-and-stick doors, which incorporate cope-and-stick joints on the grid work as well as the frame (see p. 127). Just like standard cope-and-stick router bit sets, divided-light door bits come with a matched pair of bits (and sometimes a rabbeting bit) that cut the sticking and the cope. **A** (see the bottom photo on the facing page).

1. Mill all the door parts, leaving the stiles about an inch oversized in length. Be sure to size the parts as per the router bit manufacturer's instructions. Mill the muntin and mullion stock to thickness and length, but don't rip the individual pieces to width yet. It's easier and safer to rout the cope on the end of wide blanks. Cut the mortise-and-tenon joints in

FAUX DIVIDED-LIGHT DOORS

Building a true divided-light door involves a fair amount of work due to the construction and fitting of the grid work of muntins and mullions. For a much quicker approach, you can create the look of a divided-light door by overlaying a more simply made grid work onto a single sheet of glass. The grid can be joined with half-lap joints, and then connected to the frame with mortise-and-tenon joints, dowels, pins, or even pinned miters. A single sheet of glass is then installed in a rabbet in the back of the door, just as you would a single-pane glass door.

LIGHT ILLUSION. A simple wood grid work overlaid on a single pane of glass in a door creates the effect of a divided-light door without the work of housing individual panes of glass.

COPE, THEN STICK. This router bit set for making divided-light doors includes a coping cutter (right) to cope the tenon shoulders, and a matching sticking bit (left) to cut the profile along the edges.

work SMART

Some divided-light router bit sets rely on the relatively small coped areas on the ends of muntins and mullions to hold the grid work together. Unfortunately, this doesn't provide much strength. Instead, look for sets that let you cut mortise-and-tenon joints in these areas for a longer-lasting connection.

COPE IT WIDE. For safer and easier coping of the grid pieces, work with blanks that have not yet been ripped into individual pieces. Use a backup block to guide the work past the bit, orienting the stock face down on the table.

STICK IT IN A JIG. Rout the sticking on the narrow grid pieces using a simple jig. A plywood cover and a notched end let you push the work safely past the bit with the stock face down.

the door frame (as well as the grid pieces, if your bit set allows for this).

2. Set up the coping bit in the router table, adjusting it just to touch the face of a tenon. Cope the outward facing shoulders of all the tenons, making sure to feed the stock face down on the table. **A** Then rip all the grid pieces to finished width on the tablesaw.

3. Install the sticking bit, referencing its height so it aligns with one of the coped tenons. Rout the

sticking in the rails, stiles, and grid pieces, again placing the stock face down on the table. To rout the grid pieces safely, make a simple jig to carry the parts securely past the bit. **B & C**

4. Finish the joinery work by installing a rabbeting bit in the table and routing a rabbet in the back of the stock, this time with the parts face up. **D** Use the same jig to feed the grid pieces, routing a rabbet in one edge of each piece, then tacking on a strip

RABBET THE BACK. Rout a rabbet in the back of all the parts using a bearing-guided rabbet bit, this time running the stock face up on the table.

BRING IT TOGETHER. Glue and clamp the door, first joining the grid work to the rails and then adding the stiles. Once the glue dries, trim the horns flush with the end of the door.

THE REAL DEAL. True divided-light doors have discrete rabbeted sections on the back that receive individual panes of glass.

of wood to fill that rabbet and rabbeting the opposite edge.

5. Assemble the door. The "horns" created by the excess stile length aid assembly and reduce the chances of splitting. They can be trimmed flush with the rails after glue-up. Keep in mind that you'll have to chisel away some of the fillets in the sticking at the horn area for the door joints to close fully. **E**

6. The completed door displays beautifully coped intersections where the muntins meet the mullions. The back reveals the door's authentic division of lights with its individual rabbeted areas. **F** Fit these areas with glass, and then secure the glass with adhesive, putty, or wood strips.

INSIDE FIRST. The first step in assembling the door is to glue up the half-lap grid-work joints.

STRIPS AT BACK. To hold the panels in place, install the L-shaped backer strips in the rabbet around the door's perimeter, and press the T-shape strips into the grooves in the muntins and mullions.

Shoji-Style Divided-Light Door

An alternative to a cope-and-stick divided-light door is a door more in tune with the Japanese shoji style, which consists of a simple grid work inside the frame without any profiled edges. With shoji, you have the option of filling the openings with something besides glass, such as wood, cloth, paper (used in traditional shoji), mica, and many other materials.

1. Mill the door frame parts and cut all the corner joints.

2. Make the grid work pieces, cutting tenons on the ends of all the parts, and milling a ⅛-in.-wide by ⅛-in.-deep groove in the back of each piece on the tablesaw. Cut half-lap joints at each grid intersection, and then glue up the grid work. **A**

3. Glue the assembled grid work into the door frame, and glue up the door.

4. Make wooden backer strips to hold the lights in place. L-shaped rabbeted backer strips run around the perimeter of the grid work. On each end of opposing strips (left and right, for example), cut a stub tenon that will tuck into the rabbet of the adjacent strip at the corner of the frame. For the muntin and mullion backers, rabbet stock to create T-shaped strips that will fit into the grooves you cut earlier. Make sure the tongues are deep enough to allow for the thickness of your panes or panels. Cut stub tenons on the ends where the strips intersect with each other and the door frame.

5. Insert the panels in the door, and install the backer strips into the grooves and rabbets. **B** Finish by pinning the strips into the grooves in the grid work and the rabbets in the back of the door with brads. **C**

DIVIDED-LIGHT CONSTRUCTION

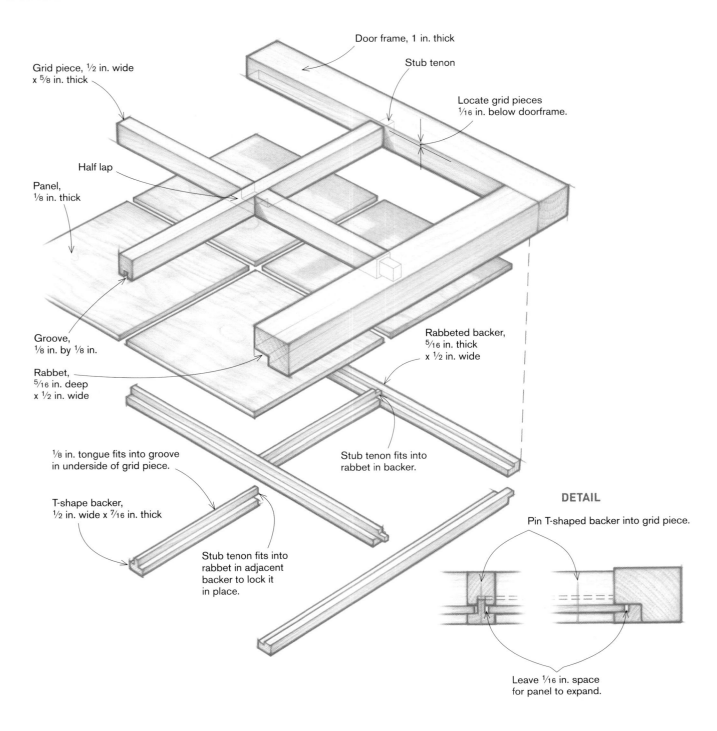

Door frame, 1 in. thick

Stub tenon

Grid piece, ½ in. wide
x ⅝ in. thick

Locate grid pieces
1/16 in. below doorframe.

Half lap

Panel,
⅛ in. thick

Groove,
⅛ in. by ⅛ in.

Rabbet,
5/16 in. deep
x ½ in. wide

Rabbeted backer,
5/16 in. thick
x ½ in. wide

⅛ in. tongue fits into groove
in underside of grid piece.

T-shape backer,
½ in. wide x 7/16 in. thick

Stub tenon fits into
rabbet in backer.

Stub tenon fits into
rabbet in adjacent
backer to lock it
in place.

DETAIL

Pin T-shaped backer into grid piece.

Leave 1/16 in. space
for panel to expand.

C

PIN THE JOINTS. Once all the strips are positioned, pin through them and into the rabbets in the doors and the grooves in the grid work, making sure the brad penetrates the center of each grid joint.

D

SLIDING PAPER AND WOOD. The deep grid work provides a convenient handhold. The upper panels, made from handmade paper glued to heavy cardboard, complement the grain-matched cherry panels below.

6. The relatively deep grid work on the assembled doors offers a handhold for sliding the doors opened or closed, and the play of wood with paper adds a distinctive touch. **D**

Arched-Top Door

Creating a simple arch at the top of a frame-and-panel door is easier than you might think. Start with a full-size drawing that includes the curve of the top rail. It's best to keep the radius larger than 10 in. to avoid short grain where the rail's shoulders meet the stiles.

1. Mill all the door parts and cut the corner joints while the stock is still square.

2. Lay out the desired curve on the top rail using a large compass **A** or a trammel—which is simply a long stick of wood with a screw tip at one end and a pencil at the other.

3. Saw the arch on the bandsaw, and then clean up the curve with a spindle sander or by hand.

4. Set up a fence on the router table and install a bearing-guided, ¼-in. slot cutter in the router, then rout the panel grooves in the straight pieces. To rout the groove in the arched rail, remove the fence, and make sure to begin the cut safely by guiding the work against a starting pin. **B**

work
SMART

Boatbuilding loans us the term *fair curve* to describe a bend that's even and consistent along its length. You can gauge a fair curve by scrutinizing the piece at eye level for any small bumps or dips. Fingers run over the curve will also quickly discern any irregularities, easily corrected with a little judicious sanding.

DRAW A CURVE. Set the compass to the desired radius and swing it along the stock, adjusting the pointed end until the pencil end aligns with both inside corners of the rail.

GROOVE IT WITH A SLOT CUTTER. Begin the cut safely by pivoting the work against a starting pin. Once the work engages the bearing, move off the pin and rout the groove by moving the work from right to left.

5. Use the same layout method to mark the curve at the top of the panel, increasing the radius by an amount equal to the depth of the groove you cut in the rail. Bandsaw and smooth the curve as before, then raise the panel on the router table using a bearing-guided panel-raising bit and a starting pin. **C**

6. Assemble the door. The panel should slide easily into the grooves in the frame without rattling. **D**

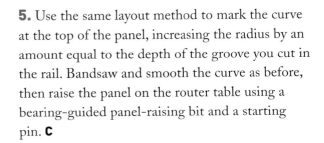

RAISE IT UPSIDE DOWN. Position the panel face down and initiate the cut with the door registered against the starting pin. Then follow the bearing to raise the curved edge.

TEST THE FIT. Dry-fit the door first, making sure the panel slides easily in the grooves and the rail shoulders meet without gaps. Then glue and clamp.

work SMART

Always raise a panel on the router table by taking incrementally deeper cuts. Otherwise, you'll stress the router and bit, and invite kickback. Begin with the bit set low for the first cut, and then raise it in small increments until you reach the desired profile. Take a light cut for the last pass, removing about 1/32 in. for a super-smooth finish that needs minimal sanding.

When making a
cabinet with a
curved door, it's
best to construct
the doors first,
then build the case
to match the door
curve.

Coopered Doors

Introducing curves into your work is a surefire way
to make an ordinary cabinet stand above the crowd,
and nowhere will a curve be more visible than on a
door or set of doors. Coopered doors offer the same
beautiful curve as other curved doors, but can be
made with a lot less fuss. That's because you begin
with flat, rectangular slats, or staves, of wood glued
edge to edge. The trick is to bevel the edges of the
staves, then glue them together on top of a curved
form to create the curve.

1. Make a full-size drawing of the curve to determine the correct bevel angle on each stave, and then
rip the bevels on the tablesaw with the blade tilted
to the appropriate angle.

2. Build a form from plywood equal to the inside
door curve, and glue the staves together on the
form using bar and web clamps. **A**

3. Once the glue has cured, smooth the outside of
the panel with a small plane, working the high spots
until the surface is one continuous curve. **B**

4. If you want a smooth curve on the inner door
face, work a sharp card scraper diagonally across the
grain. **C** Alternatively, it's okay to leave the inside
faceted.

5. Construct the case, and then hang the door,
making sure to leave enough room for wood movement, since you're building a form of slab door. One
creative option is to cut coves on the outside of the
staves before gluing them together to create a scalloped face on the outside, which helps hide the glue
joints. **D & E**

STAVES MAKE A PANEL. Apply glue to all the mating edges, and draw
the staves tightly together and down against the form using bar and
web clamps.

PLANE THE OUTSIDE. A block plane makes quick work of removing
the stave ridges to create a smooth, continuous surface on the
door face.

SCRAPE THE INSIDE. Work the scraper diagonally at first
to level the high spots, then finish by scraping and sanding
with the grain.

COVES HIDE THE JOINTS. Chris Tomasi coved the staves on the front of his coopered-door cabinet before glue-up, adding a scalloped effect while sidestepping the issue of smoothing the glued-up face.

Curved Frame-and-Panel Doors

More complex to make than coopered doors, laminated doors offer greater design freedom, letting you create frames and panels from continuous sheets of wood, or laminates, preserving grain pattern, color, and texture. A laminated door consists of multiple layers of thin wood pressed together over a curved form. The plies can be oriented either in the same grain direction or cross-grained, like plywood. The result is a rail, stile, or panel that's more dimensionally stable than solid wood—a plus for any construction.

The laminating technique is the same as when making drawers with curved fronts (see p. 75). One approach is to use a two-part form to press the laminates together. An easier alternative is to bend the work over a one-part form, pressing everything in a vacuum bag. For wide panels, you can add cross-plies of the same wood to create cross-grain laminates. If the panel's edges will be concealed in a frame, you can use bending plywood for the interior plies. Either way, you're basically creating your own dimensionally stable plywood.

CURVED ROUTING. Clamp a curved fence to the router table, and cut the curved groove with a straight bit as you slide the work against the fence.

CURVING IN. These gently bowed doors feature bent-laminated panels rabbeted to fit in grooves in the bent-laminated frame rails.

work SMART

You can save a lot of lamination work by cutting curved rails from solid stock. Just draw the desired curve on stock thick enough to accommodate it, and then cut to your lines using the bandsaw. Some would argue that the resulting grain pattern will not be as elegant as grain on the face of bent stock, but if you keep the curvature slight, the overall effect will be successful.

1. Make a full-size drawing of the curved door parts, including the rails and panel. Build the curved bending forms you'll need by referring to your drawings. Then cut the laminates and glue up the rails and the panel to create the desired curves.

2. Cut the mortises in the stiles as usual. Then lay out the angled tenons on the curved rails, and cut to your lines on the bandsaw.

3. Groove the stiles in the normal fashion, and then set up a curved fence on the router table to rout the curved grooves in the rails. **A**

4. Trim the panel to size, and then rabbet the convex face to fit the grooves in the frame, using a dado blade on the tablesaw or a straight bit on the router table. It's not that tricky: Just keep the panel in contact with the table at the cutting point.

5. Assemble the door, gluing the corner joints only.

6. Fit and hang the door. Depending on your preference, you can make a door with a convex face that bows outward or a concave door (or pair of doors) that curves gently inward. **B**

Curved Glass-Faceted Door

This curved door, built by furniture maker Gary van Rawlins, is also constructed with bent-laminated rails. However, this one houses a series of flat glass panes that sit in faceted rabbets in the rails, giving the illusion of a curved glass door. It's best to make a full-size drawing of the rail so you can accurately calculate the rabbets.

1. Build the curved frame as described previously. Note that with this style of door, you have the option of creating an elliptical curve instead of an arc of a circle. Again, make full-size patterns of the rails, including the faceted rabbets.

ROUT A RABBET. Make a thick plywood template of the facet configuration, then clamp the rail to the template to rout the faceted rabbet using with a pattern bit.

A

BEGIN AT THE EDGES. Install the glass in the door by first slipping the outermost panels into the stile grooves.

2. Groove both stiles to accommodate ⅛-in.-thick glass, then cut the faceted rabbets in each rail. Include small flats between the facets to serve as bearing surfaces for the ends of the vertical dividers. Rout the rabbets using a pattern bit, which is a straight bit with a bearing between the cutting flute and the shank. Guide the bit against a plywood template of the facets made from your drawing, clamping the template to the rail. **A**

3. Glue and assemble the frame.

4. Make a series of vertical dividers to fit between the rabbets on the top and bottom of the door. Groove both edges to accept the glass, and cut a stub tenon at each end to sit in the rabbet.

5. Measure the openings and the faceted areas of the rabbet, taking into account the flat bearing surfaces for the divider tenons, and have a glass shop cut the glass panes slightly smaller than the opening sizes.

6. Install the glass in the door by starting with the outermost panes, slipping them into the grooves in the stiles. **B**

B

MOVE TO THE MIDDLE. Install the last two panes and the center divider by lifting upward slightly. Once the divider is in place, lower the assembly onto the rabbets.

7. Add another pane, and then slip a divider onto its edge, and so on until you reach the middle. Install the last central divider by lifting the panes upward slightly until the divider slips onto both panes. **C**

8. Finish up by making two retaining strips for the top and bottom rabbets. You can lay out the strips to match the facets in the rabbets, and cut them on the bandsaw or use a jig similar to the one you used for the rabbets. Install the retainers over the panes and dividers, pinning them into the rail rabbet. **D**

9. The completed door is actually an ellipse, which is a more interesting curve than a conventional radius. **E**

TWO STRIPS ARE ALL YOU NEED. Fit the faceted retainer strips into the top and bottom rabbets to secure the glass and the divider. Pin it to the rails with brads.

ACCELERATED CURVE. The finished door has elliptical rails, in which a smaller radius at one edge accelerates into a larger curve at the opposite edge.

Beads, Inlay, and Other Decorative Effects

Profiling the inside edges of your door frames with roundovers, ogees (such as those found on a typical cope-and-stick door), stopped chamfers, or even a simple bead boosts a door's appeal. You'll need to plane or rout the profile on the frame pieces before assembling the door, making sure to cut any miters at the corners if necessary. If you're using a veneered panel, which is dimensionally stable, you can cut the profile on the edges of the panel instead, which simplifies the joinery.

In addition to adding shaped parts to the frame or panel, you can opt for the traditional approach of inlaying contrasting veneer into the surface, whether it's a simple line of string inlay or banding or a more complex panel of marquetry.

You can buy string inlay, which is simply thin strips of veneer, or make your own by sawing solid wood into narrow strips. You can also buy banding, which is made from various pieces of veneer arranged in different patterns and glued together to form a somewhat wider strip. Crossbanding is a specific type of banding in which the majority of the grain of the veneer runs 90 degrees to its length, often used along edges to provide contrast. To install banding or string inlay, use a small-diameter straight bit in a router, setting the depth slightly less than the thickness of the veneer, then guiding the router against a straightedge to rout a channel. Spread glue in the channel, press the inlay in place,

BEADED AND BANDED. Before assembling the door, the author glued strips of wood to the edges of the veneered panel, which was shaped with a 3/16-in. bead and inlaid with a strip of 1/4-in.-wide crossbanding made from satinwood veneer.

and sand it flush once the glue dries. A good place to try your hand at this is the border area around a flat door panel.

Marquetry is the art of creating pictures, designs, or patterns by shaping and taping together various pieces of contrasting veneer into a sheet, then gluing and clamping the assembled sheet to the face of the door or cabinet.

Other materials beside wood can be readily inlaid into a door as well. For example, polished river stones can be incorporated into a wood panel by cutting a custom pocket for each stone and then epoxying the stone into the pocket. The effect is unique, and can make a door truly one-of-a-kind.

A PICTURE FROM PIECES. The character on the face of Marc Adams' cabinet was pieced together from contrasting veneers, and then glued to the surface of both the doors and drawers.

PILLOWS OF STONE. The author traced each stone's outline onto the panel, and then used a ball-mill bit in a rotary grinder to carve a custom-fitted pocket. Use a two-part epoxy to hold the stones in place.

Index